HOW TO cheat IN Photoshop

The art of creating photorealistic montages

Steve Caplin

Focal Press

OXFORD AMSTERDAM BOSTON LONDON NEW YORK PARIS
SAN DIEGO SAN FRANCISCO SINGAPORE SYDNEY TOKYO

Focal Press
An imprint of Elsevier Science
Linacre House, Jordan Hill, Oxford OX2 8DP
225 Wildwood Avenue, Woburn MA 01801-2041

First published 2002

British Library Cataloguing in Publication Data
A catalogue record for this book is available from the British Library

Library of Congress Cataloguing in Publication Data
A catalogue record for this book is available from the Library of Congress

ISBN 0 240 51702 4

For information on all Focal Press publications visit our website at:
www.focalpress.com

Cover images: Steve Caplin

Printed and bound in Italy

C O N T E N T S

C O N T E N T S

4 Light and shade 64

5 Heads and bodies 90

6 Shiny surfaces 114

CONTENTS

CONTENTS

10 Hyper realism 208

11 Carry on spending 232

How to cheat, and why

Why yet another book on Photoshop?

Most of the Photoshop books in print go to great lengths to explain how each tool, dialog and menu works, examining the smallest tweak of each slider and variable and discussing its effects on the image.

What they don't tend to show is how to use Photoshop to achieve a task you've been commissioned to do – specifically, how to use it to create artwork that looks as if it's been photographed.

Photorealism simply means making montages look real. Too often we'll see montages where the heads are different colors to the bodies, where there's no eye contact or interaction between a group of people stuck together in a single image. In my view this is unforgivable: few photographers would be able to earn their living producing bland, emotionless pictures, yet those creating photomontages seem to forget the most basic of rules. A picture must tell a story – which means rhythm, composition, and interaction between its constituent elements.

The truth about cheating

I've used the word 'cheating' in the title of this book in two ways. The most obvious is that I'm describing how to make images look as much as possible like photographs, when they're not. In this sense, it simply means creating photographic work without the need for a studio.

The other sense of 'cheating' is finding shortcuts to help you work more quickly and more economically. Too often you'll see Photoshop techniques explained using long-winded, complex operations that take an age to complete.

Wherever possible, I've used quicker solutions to achieve the same results. For the artist on a deadline, the difference between a perfect work of art and one that's turned in on time means the difference between a happy client and one faced with a blank page in the next day's newspaper.

Workthroughs and examples

Each workthrough in this book is designed as a double page spread. That way, you can prop the book up behind your keyboard while going through the associated file on the CD ROM. While the workthroughs are all designed to illustrate a specific technique, I've also outlined each step as a general guide to the process of creating illustrations in Photoshop. So you may find that several steps in a workthrough appear to have nothing to do with the subject of the chapter: I've just taken the opportunity to discuss other points of interest.

Some of the workthroughs take the form of case studies, where I dissect an illustration I've done as a commissioned job; many of the sections open with one of my illustrations as a real-world example of the technique I'm talking about. One reason I've used my own artwork is that I know how it was created. In many cases I've kept the original layered Photoshop files, so it's been possible for me to take the images apart and show how they were made.

There's another, more pertinent reason. Messing about in Photoshop can be the most fun you can have without breaking the law, and the novice user will experiment with filters and color changes endlessly. But it's not until you produce an illustration to a specific brief that you realize the issues and problems involved – and then find a way around them. Almost all the techniques I describe in this book have been learned out of necessity; there's nothing like a tight deadline to concentrate the mind. Adrenaline is sometimes the best drug there is.

Between each chapter you'll find an Interlude, in which I discuss an issue of relevance to the Photoshop artist. Think of them as light relief.

Screen shots and windows

Most Photoshop books use standard screen grabs as examples, which means two things: firstly, the examples are constrained to the monitor's 4:3 proportions, and secondly, an awful lot of space is taken up with frames, title bars and borders. I take the view that anyone working in Photoshop knows what a window looks like, and doesn't need to be reminded half a dozen times on every page. So except in the rare instances where I'll show a dialog box – when the settings need to be shown for a filter, for example – I've dispensed with the window frames altogether, so we can just concentrate on the images. This has also given me greater flexibility in the number and shape of the examples I include for each workthrough. Hopefully, it's also made the book more varied and interesting to look at.

What's on the CD?

I've included most of the workthroughs in this book on the CD, so that after reading about them you can open up the original Photoshop files and experiment with them for yourself. I've reduced the image sizes to make them more manageable, so you'll find yourself working with screen resolution rather than high resolution images. I've also included some movies showing specific techniques in action.

In a few cases, I haven't been able to provide the examples on the CD. These tend to be workthroughs that are case studies, in which I've used images of politicians and other celebrities for whom it was impossible to get clearance to include them for electronic distribution. All the other images have been either photographed by me or generously provided by the various image libraries concerned, to whom I owe a debt of gratitude. A credit on each page in the book indicates the source of the images that have been included on the CD. You'll also find demonstration versions of some of the third party plug-ins I've described on the CD, so go ahead and try them out. For full details of what's included, see page 248.

Spelling and metaphors

I've tried to use American spelling wherever possible. Firstly, because we're more used to reading US spelling in England than Americans are to reading English spelling; and secondly, because Photoshop is an American product. Initially I tried not to use any words that were spelled differently in the two languages, but I found it impossible to get through the book without once mentioning the word 'color'. My apologies if I've employed any phrases or vernacular that don't work on both sides of the Atlantic. It's a wide ocean, and some expressions don't survive the journey.

Going further

You'll find links to sites of interest, as well as contact details and any extra information that may come to light after this book is published, on the website at www.howtocheatinphotoshop.com – so stop by and take a look. In the meantime, enjoy the book.

Steve Caplin
London and Brighton, 2002

ACKNOWLEDGMENTS

This book is dedicated to Carol, of course, not least for looking after
Freddy and Joe while I wrote it.

I'm immeasurably grateful to the following:
Marie Hooper of Focal Press, for her patience and persistence
Martin Evening, for endless help and advice
Keith Martin, for helping me create the keyboard shortcuts font
Adam Banks, for correcting the original manuscript
Students at the University of Westminster, for asking why I hadn't written
a book about Photoshop yet
...and of course Adobe Systems, for making Photoshop in the first place.

I'm indebted to the art editors of the newspapers and magazines who
commissioned the artwork I've used as examples in this book:
Jonathan Anstee, Kevin Bayliss, Julian Bovis, Roger Browning,
Zelda Davey, Miles Dickson, Robin Hedges, Paul Howe, Lisa Irving,
Alice Ithier, Ben Jackson, Jasmina Jambresic, Vicky Jones,
Fraser McDermott, Garry Mears, John Morris, Doug Morrison,
Lawrence Morton, Martin Parfitt, Mark Porter, Stephen Reid,
Tom Reynolds, Caz Roberts and Matt Straker.

Many of the images in this book are taken from royalty-free photo
libraries. Their websites are as follows:

Bodyshots	www.digiwis.com
Corel	www.corel.com
Hemera	www.hemera.com (Digital Image Content © 1997-2002 Hemera Technologies Inc. All rights reserved.)
Photodisc	www.photodisc.com (Digital images © 2001 PhotoDisc/Getty Images)
Rubber Ball	www.rubberball.com (all images © Rubber Ball Productions)
Stockbyte	www.stockbyte.com

How to use this book

I doubt if any readers of this book are going to start at the beginning and work their way diligently through to the end. In fact, you're probably only reading this section because your computer's just crashed and you can't follow any more of the workthroughs until it's booted up again. This is the kind of book you should be able to just dip into and extract the information you need.

But I'd like to make a couple of recommendations. The first two chapters, Natural Selection and Hiding and Showing, deal with the basics of photomontage. There are many Photoshop users who have never learnt how to use the Pen tool, or picked up the essential keyboard shortcuts; I frequently meet experienced users who have never quite figured out how to use layer masks. Because I talk about these techniques throughout the book, I need to bring everyone up to speed before we get onto the harder stuff. So my apologies if I start off by explaining things you already know: it'll get more interesting later on.

Each chapter is effectively a self-contained unit, but the techniques do build up as you progress through the workthroughs. Frequently, I'll use a technique that's been discussed in more detail earlier in the same chapter, so it may be worth going through the pages in each chapter in order, even if you don't read every chapter in the book.

  A CD icon on a page indicates that the Photoshop file for that workthrough is on the CD, so you can open it up and try it out for yourself. The Movie icon indicates that there's a QuickTime movie on the CD that shows the workthrough acted out.

At the beginning of each chapter you'll find a visual index that shows a thumbnail representing the theme of each workthrough. It's there to help you find my exploration of a technique you've already read but which you can't remember the title of, and I hope it's helpful.

1 Natural selection

THE TECHNIQUES described in this book assume you have a reasonable working knowledge of Photoshop. In later chapters, we'll discuss ways of working that involve modifying selections, and using both QuickMask and the Pen tool to create Bézier curves. The first part of this chapter will serve as a refresher course on these fundamental techniques for those who already know them, and will introduce the concepts for those who have not yet experimented with them.

Later in the chapter, we'll go into more detail on how to work with and modify layers and colors without having to pick up a brush first: there are many techniques, such as those for changing colors selectively, that can be accomplished entirely by means of dialog boxes.

Selection: the fundamentals

1 Normal drawing with the Marquee tool is from corner to corner. But if you're using the Elliptical Marquee, it's hard to conceive of where the imaginary corner might be. Hold down ⌥ *alt* *after* you begin drawing to draw from the center outwards. The selected region is shown at the side.

2 If you hold ⌥ *alt* *before* you draw a second selection, you will remove this selection from the original one. Be sure to press the modifier key before you begin drawing, or you'll simply draw from the center. Here, we've deselected the center of the hubcap, leaving just the rim.

ALL PHOTOSHOP WORK begins with making selections. Shown here are some of the basic keyboard shortcuts that every Photoshop user should be able to use as second nature: even if you hate learning keyboard commands, you owe it to your productivity and your sanity to learn these.

Temporarily accessing the Move tool, using the shortcut shown in step 8, works when any other tool is active – not just the selection tools. This makes it easy to move any layer around while painting, selecting or using type, without having to reach for the toolbar.

6 If you find holding down all these keys in sequence hard to get to grips with, consider using QuickMask instead.

To access it, simply type **Q** and you'll go into QuickMask mode – see overleaf for how to make QuickMask display the selection rather than its inverse.

The QuickMask equivalents of the selected areas defined in steps 1 to 5 are shown beneath each step. Selected areas are overlaid in red; unselected areas remain colorless, making it easy to see exactly where your final selection will be. The mask corresponds precisely to the selection area, as can be seen in the examples on this page.

7 If you drag a selected area with a selection tool active (Marquee, Lasso etc), you'll move the selected region but not its contents.

3 Holding ⎇ *alt* subtracts from the selection, but holding *Shift* adds to it. Again, be sure to hold the modifier before you begin drawing. By holding this key down, we're able to add back the middle knob on the hubcap from the section we'd previously deselected.

4 Here's what happens if we combine the two keys. Holding ⎇ *Shift* *alt* *Shift* intersects the new selection with the previous one, resulting in just the overlap between the two. Here, the original elliptical selection is intersected with the new rectangular selection.

5 A little-known modifier is the Space bar, which performs a unique task: it allows you to move a selection while you're drawing it, which is of enormous benefit when selecting areas such as the ellipse of the hubcap. Here, we've used the technique to move the selection over to the side.

8 To access the Move tool temporarily, hold ⌘ *ctrl* before you drag. Now, the selection itself will be moved when you drag it.

9 Holding down ⎇ *alt* as well will move a copy, leaving the original selection where it was – but be sure to hold the modifier before dragging.

10 You can continue to make several copies by releasing and holding the mouse button while holding the ⎇ *alt* key down.

SHORTCUTS
MAC WIN BOTH

5

QuickMask: better selectivity

Quick Mask Options

Color Indicates:
- ⭕ Masked Areas
- 🔘 Selected Areas

OK

Cancel

Color

Opacity: 50 %

1 This array of dots was created by entering QuickMask, drawing a circle, and using `⌥` `Delete` `alt` `Delete` to fill with the foreground color (black), which shows up as red. The array is made simply by nudging the selection.

QUICKMASK IS THE MOST POWERFUL tool for creating selections in Photoshop. The default setting is for QuickMask to show the masked (unselected) areas with a red overlay, leaving the selected areas transparent: I find it far preferable to work the other way around, so that the selected areas are highlighted. To change the settings, you need to double-click the QuickMask icon (near the bottom of the toolbar, just below the foreground/background color swatches) and use the settings shown above.

Entering QuickMask is easy: simply type the letter Q, and use the same key to leave. The power of QuickMask lies in the fact that you can use any of the painting tools, as well as the selection tools, to define your selection areas. This means you can easily create partly feathered regions as well as hard edges, ellipses and curves, all within the same selection.

QuickMask operates in much the same way as layer masks, so see Chapter 3 for more ideas on how this works.

4 In this example, I've used the Gradient tool to draw a simple gradient from right to left: the right-hand side will then be fully selected, fading away to the left which is completely deselected.

7 Here, I've used the Brush tool to paint a soft line across the eyebrows. This is the equivalent of drawing with the Lasso tool, and then feathering the selection; but it's a far more controllable way of selecting the area we want.

2 When we leave QuickMask, here's what we see: an array of circular selections, perfectly aligned in a way that would have been almost impossible if we'd tried to draw it simply using the Elliptical Marquee tool on its own.

3 We can now do anything we like with that selection. Here, I've simply inverted it to show how smoothly the ellipses blend with the background image.

5 Leaving QuickMask, we see what appears to be a simple rectangular selection on the right. This is because the selection marquee can't display graduated areas: the dotted line down the center marks the 50% selection threshold.

6 I've now applied the Color Halftone filter to the selection. Notice how the filter fades away smoothly from right to left: the filter is only applied at the strength of the selected area.

8 When we exit QuickMask we can see that, once again, the selection marquee is incapable of showing the true scope of the selected area, showing the 50% threshold region instead.

9 Moving a copy of the selected area up, we can see that there's no hard line where the two pairs of eyebrows meet. Selecting using the combination of Brush and QuickMask is the best way of making soft-edged selections.

HOT TIP

As well as the selection and painting tools, you can use many of the filters in QuickMask as well. It's even possible to use the Free Transform tool, and there's no need to make a selection first – the mask will automatically be the area to be transformed. This is particularly useful for selecting elliptical areas of an image that aren't strictly vertical or horizontal.

SHORTCUTS

The Pen is mightier. . .

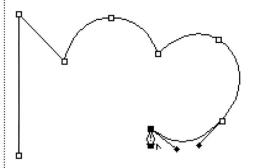

THE PEN TOOL is one of the key tools available to the illustrator – not just in Photoshop but in Illustrator, FreeHand and many other programs as well.

The Pen tool creates paths using Bézier curves (named after the French designer who devised them, so legend has it, to design the outline of the Citroen 2CV in the 1930s). Bézier curves are unique in that simple curves can be made to fit any shape: they're easily editable after they've been drawn, so you needn't worry about getting the curve perfect first time around – it can always be adjusted later.

The paths created by the Pen tool have another great advantage: they can be used to define selections which can then be stored within the document when it's saved. Most of the cutout objects in royalty-free CD collections are defined with paths.

The problem is that the Pen tool has the steepest learning curve of all. Here, and on the following pages, I'll try to help you get to grips with mastering the essential tool for making perfect selections.

1 To draw straight lines with the Pen tool, simply click each point. If you want to constrain a line to horizontal, vertical or 45°, hold down the **Shift** key before clicking the second point.

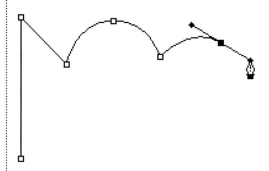

4 Because we clicked and didn't drag in step 3, when the next point is drawn (with a click and drag), the curve coming out of the back of it joins the previous one with a hard corner rather than a smooth curve.

7 If you've clicked and dragged on a point, making a smooth curve, you can turn it into a corner point instead by holding **⌥ alt** and clicking on the point again. You can then click and drag on the same point again to make a new curve from that corner.

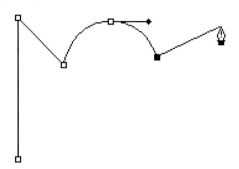

2 If you click and then drag before releasing the button, you'll get a curve. This is the essence of the Pen tool: curves are defined by the anchor points (the dots where you click) and the handles that set their direction and strength.

3 Every time you click and drag, you get a curve; and the point clicked in the previous step shows how the curve operates on both sides of the point. But if you just click without dragging, you make a corner point.

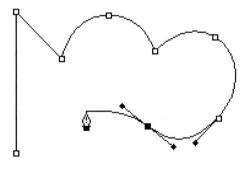

5 The handles operate as tangents to the curve, not crossing it but acting like a surface off which the curve bounces. The points should be placed at positions where the curve changes direction.

6 Sometimes, the handles do appear to cross the curve - but only in cases where the curve is S-shaped, as appears here. The handles are still really tangents to each side of the curve.

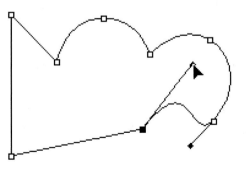

8 When you click on the starting point again, the path will be completed and the anchor points will disappear, showing just the path's outline. You can leave a path open-ended instead, if you like – for example, if you want to stroke it with a painting tool (see Pipes and Cables in Chapter 9).

9 A path can be adjusted by moving the anchor points, moving the handles, or dragging on the curve itself. Hold ⌘ ctrl to move points with the Pen tool active; or press **A** for the path selection tool – use the filled tool to select an entire path, the hollow version for individual points.

HOT TIP

You don't need to wait until completing a path before making adjustments to it: simply hold ⌘ ctrl at any point while you're drawing to access the path selection tool, and use it to move anchor points or their handles. When you release the key, you can just carry on drawing.

Putting the Pen into practice

1 Begin by clicking the first point just below the mug's handle, then click and drag down a short way at the bottom of the straight section.

2 Now click and drag at the bottom of the curve: keep your drag horizontal, so it makes a tangent to the curve.

O N THE PREVIOUS PAGE we looked at the basics of using the Pen tool. Here's a short workthrough to take you through the process of outlining a simple object: you'll find the image on the CD that accompanies this book, so you can try it out for yourself.

This is a compound path, in that it includes one element within another. You don't need to do anything to the path within the handle to make it subtract from the main outline: Photoshop will take care of this automatically.

6 Complete this small curve by clicking and dragging just around the corner. Keep the drag parallel to the mug once more.

7 Now click and drag at the middle of the top of the mug. This is the mid-point of the curve that makes the mug rim.

11 Click and drag at the point on the handle where the curve changes direction – just around from the top.

12 Another click and drag, once again where the direction of the curve changes, on the outermost part of the handle.

3 Go round the corner, and click and drag a short way up the side of the mug. Drag the handle so that it follows the line of the mug.

4 Now click at the top of the straight section, and drag a short distance to create the start of the curve that follows.

5 Click and drag at the beginning of the lip at the top of the mug: only a short drag is needed to make this curve.

8 Click and drag again at the edge of the rim, just before the lip curve begins.

9 Now click and drag once more just around the lip, again keeping the drag parallel to the side of the mug.

10 Now click at the top of the handle, but don't drag this time: there's a sharp corner here, and we don't want a curve at this point.

13 Click on the starting point and drag into the mug – it's the back of the handle that defines the curve behind it.

14 Follow the same process to make the inside of the handle, remembering to make corner points where the handle joins the mug.

15 With the path complete, you can turn it into a selection using ⌘ Enter ctrl Enter; inverse the selection and delete the background.

HOT TIP

Don't worry if the curves you draw don't match the mug first time: you can always adjust them later, either by dragging on the curve itself or by dragging an anchor point or handle.
You can also edit the anchor points themselves: when you click the Pen tool on an active path, you'll create a new anchor point at that position, but if you click on an existing anchor point you'll delete it.

SHORTCUTS

MAC WIN BOTH

11

Losing the edges

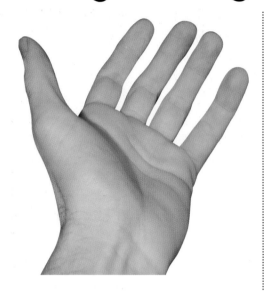

WHETHER YOU ISOLATE AN OBJECT from its background using the Magic Wand tool, or by loading a pre-drawn path, you'll frequently find a slight fringe of the background color surrounding the layer. This is due to the anti-aliasing technique used in Photoshop to ensure a smooth edge.

There are two built-in methods for removing this fringe – Defringe and Remove White Matte. Neither does the job perfectly; here, we'll look at the effects of both these techniques, and at a couple of extra methods that I find work more effectively.

All these techniques assume that the cutout object – the hand, in this case – is on a separate layer from the background.

1 When placed against a complex background such as this foliage, the white fringe on the hand is hard to discern: there's so much visual detail going on behind it that the eye is distracted.

4 The next alternative is Remove White Matte, also found in the Matting menu. Once again, this gets rid of the white area automatically, but tends to result in an unnaturally dark edge on the remaining pixels.

2 Placed against a plain background, we can now see the white fringe more clearly. The lower picture, detailing the tip of the forefinger, shows an enlarged view of the image so that we can see the effect of the different operations we're about to perform.

3 The first method of removing the white is Defringe, found under Layer/Matting. Entering a figure of 1 pixel in the dialog removes the white by sampling the colors just inside the radius specified, and pushing those colors outwards to replace those already there. It gets rid of the white, but is a little clumsy: we tend to get hard blocks of unwanted color this way.

5 My preferred method is to load the layer's selection by ⌘ *ctrl* clicking on the name in the Layers palette, inversing the selection using ⌘ *Shift* *I* *ctrl* *Shift* *I* and then deleting – which has the effect of removing a single pixel from all the way round the image. To save time, you can write an Action to perform this task with a single keystroke – see the Interlude at the end of Chapter 6.

6 There are times when deleting a pixel all the way round doesn't work – if the elements on the layer are particularly fine, for example. In these cases, you need to take a more painstaking approach: lock the transparency of the layer using *I* and then, using a small soft-edged brush, paint around the edge of the layer, sampling the adjacent colors with the Eyedropper tool frequently as you go.

HOT TIP

The method outlined in step 6 works well for layers of a uniform color range, such as skin tones. But if you're working on a complex patterned layer such as textiles, the painted edge will look false. The alternative here is to use the Cloning tool, sampling just inside the edge as you work your way round.

SHORTCUTS
MAC WIN BOTH

Lock and load

LOCKING TRANSPARENCY is an essential capability to learn, as it allows you to paint on a layer without affecting transparent areas. It's a feature we'll be using throughout this book.

Loading selection areas is another shortcut that you'll see used again and again in the chapters that follow, and it's important to understand how it works. In the example here, we're working on a document that includes three playing cards, on separate layers. We want to create a shadow on a fourth layer, above the other three: by loading up the transparency of the underlying card layers, we can achieve our aim with ease. It's worth noting that the shortcuts for adding to and subtracting from selections are the same as those used for standard selections, as described earlier in this chapter.

1 Under normal conditions, when we paint on a layer the paint will be applied irrespective of the layer's boundaries, as can be seen here.

2 If we check the Lock Transparency box on the Layers palette, any painting actions are limited to those pixels already present in the layer: they change color, but aren't added to.

1 To begin with, let's load up the Queen of Hearts layer by holding ⌘ *ctrl* and clicking on the name in the Layers palette. The outlines show that area selected.

2 We want to add the Jack of Diamonds, so now we need an extra modifier key: holding ⌘ *Shift* *ctrl* *Shift* and clicking on the name will add that to the existing selection.

3 So what, you might think. Well, here's a typical example: we want to change the color of this woman's dull jacket into something a little more eye-catching.

4 With the Brush tool set to Color mode, we'd expect the color of the jacket to change without affecting the texture. But the color leaks out, polluting the background as well.

5 Once we lock the transparency of the pixels, we can paint our color directly onto the layer without affecting the rest of the artwork: again, only the pixels present are affected.

3 We only want to work on the two back cards, so we need to subtract the Five of Hearts layer. Holding ⎇ ⌘ *alt* *ctrl* while clicking on the name removes that layer's selection.

4 With our selection made, we can now make a new layer for the shadow and begin to paint – hiding the selection edges first (⌘ H *ctrl* H) so we can see what we're doing.

5 But the Jack has to cast a shadow on the Queen as well. Holding ⎇ ⌘ *alt* *ctrl* while clicking on its name will remove the Jack's selection, and we can add the shadow we want.

HOT TIP

The shortcut for locking and unlocking transparency is ⦸. The trouble is, this is also the shortcut for locking a layer so it can't be painted on, and locking it so it can't be moved. In general, the key will repeat the last action you chose by clicking in the icons on the palette; but if you do find yourself getting a warning that a task couldn't be completed, just go to the palette and uncheck the box.

SHORTCUTS
MAC WIN BOTH

15

Find and replace

1 The brash blue of this once-elegant Victorian building may not appeal to all tastes. It certainly doesn't appeal to mine, so let's change it to something more environmentally friendly. Choose Image/Adjust/Replace Color to get started.

CHANGING THE COLOR of the car above from red to blue would be an almost impossible task by conventional means: all those railings in the way would make selecting the car something of a nightmare. But by using Replace Color, we can adjust the hue selectively without having to lay hands on a single selection or painting tool.

Replace Color is a hugely powerful tool that turns what would otherwise be a complex task into one that's enjoyable and fun.

4 To add more colors, hold the **Shift** key and click on an unchanged area, or drag to select a range of colors: that range will be added to the selection, and the color will change in the image. If you select a spot by accident, hold **⌥ alt** while clicking to deselect that color.

2 By default, the Replace Color dialog shows a monochrome view of what's been selected: white is active, black isn't. By clicking on the image, regions of that color become selected. When you change the Hue value, the image changes to reflect that, as seen in the next step.

3 Here's the result of our initial change, and we're turning the building green. It doesn't matter what color you choose to begin with; go for something bright, so you can see the change. So far, only a portion of the face of the building has changed color.

5 Keep adding more color ranges until the entire building is altered. One way of increasing the range of colors changed is to raise the Fuzziness value; but this draws in unwanted colors in the surrounding area, as can be seen in the color change in the windows of the neighboring building.

6 Now we're sure the building is selected, we can change the hue to a shade more in keeping with its surroundings. It may not be painted white like the building to the left of it, but it certainly blends into the street better than it did before.

HOT TIP

There are often areas in the surrounding image that are close to the target color range, and they will get changed as well. One solution is to duplicate the layer, apply Replace Color, and then simply erase or mask the parts you didn't want to change.

SHORTCUTS
MAC WIN BOTH

17

Color by numbers

1 This image shows a complex skyline, with many fiddly elements punctuating the heavens – from the street light to the strings of bulbs stretched between them, to the ornate roof on the building on the left. An impossible job using the Lasso tool: but there's a better way. Choose Select/Color Range to begin the operation.

T HE SELECT COLOR COMMAND works in precisely the same way as the Replace Color dialog detailed on the previous page, except that rather than changing the hue it returns a selection.

This makes it the ideal tool for changing elements such as the sky, as shown in this example: with the sky isolated from the original image, we can paste in any cloud formation we want to strengthen and add drama to the image. Here, we've taken a sunny day on the Brighton seafront and made the scene altogether more doom-laden simply by replacing the sky with something a touch more dramatic.

3 With the sky selected, open any other sky you have lying around and paste it inside the selected area: use `Shift` `⌘` `V` `Shift` `ctrl` `V` or choose Paste Into from the Edit menu. The new sky will be positioned within the selection, and you can move or scale it as required; it will move independently of the area you've just pasted it inside.

2 The dialog works in the same way as Replace Color: the main difference is that the selected area is shown on the image as a QuickMask selection, although you can change this using the pop-up menu. Use *Shift* and *alt* as before, to add and subtract colors to and from the selected range, until the entire sky is selected.

4 Choosing Paste Into creates a layer mask that exactly matches the original selection – see Chapter 2 for more about how to use layer masks. We can now paint on the mask to remove pieces of sky from regions where it shouldn't have appeared, such as halfway up the railings on the left. We'll also take this opportunity to adjust the foreground image to match the new sky's colors.

HOT TIP

If you've performed a Select Color operation and want to repeat it exactly, hold *alt* as you select it again from the menu. It will reappear with the same settings already loaded up. Holding this modifier will reload the last settings for any of the color adjustments as well.

SHORTCUTS
MAC WIN BOTH

The perfect set-up

GETTING THE BEST OUT OF PHOTOSHOP means making the application behave the way you want it to. This may mean investing in memory and additional hard disk space, as well as taking care arranging your palettes.

Photoshop needs as much memory as you can give it. RAM is cheaper now than it has ever been: if you're serious about Photoshop, you should be looking at a total system RAM configuration of at least 512Mb – more if you can manage it. The more real RAM (rather than Virtual Memory) Photoshop has available to it, the faster it will run.

Even with enormous amounts of RAM, Photoshop will still write huge temporary files. It deletes these when you quit the application, so you're unlikely to notice them, but they can run into hundreds of megabytes. If your main hard disk is used as a 'scratch disk' Photoshop will be reduced to fitting these files in whatever spaces it can find; they'll be so fragmented that the whole process will become slowed down.

The best solution is to buy a second hard disk of at least 4Gb in size, or partition a larger disk, and assign this to be Photoshop's scratch disk – you do this using File / Preferences / Plug-ins and Scratch Disks. Resist the temptation to put anything else on this disk: keeping a large, clean disk spare for the exclusive use of Photoshop will greatly speed up its processing power (to say nothing of reducing fragmentation on your main hard drive).

Even with a clean scratch disk, Photoshop will still have to wade through its large temporary files, particularly if you're working on big images. Get into the habit of using the Purge All command (Edit menu) every time you're sure you won't want to undo what you've just done, use the History palette or paste an item from the clipboard. This will clear out the temporary files, and can often take a minute or so to accomplish – which gives you some idea of how large these files can get.

You can set up your frequently used palettes by storing them in the Palette Well, so they can be accessed with a single click; they'll also vanish when you

If there are graphic elements, such
as logos, that you use frequently,
define them as custom shapes and
they'll always be ready to hand.

Store your frequently used palettes
in the Palette Well. They'll appear
when you click on them, and
disappear when you've finished.

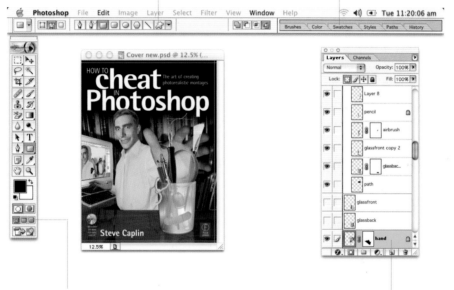

Click an icon to see the image alone
against a gray background, or against
black with menus hidden: use the F key
to cycle through the options.

Don't store the Layers palette in the
Palette Well – you'll need this
constantly on view.

click elsewhere. But if you want to see the image you're working on uncluttered
by any screen debris, press the Tab key and all the palettes, including the
Toolbar and Options bar, will disappear. Press the Tab key once more to bring
them back. Don't put the Layers palette into the Palette Well, since you won't
want that to keep disappearing, and there's no need to put the File Browser here
– you can open that with a keyboard shortcut.

If you're working on complex montages that contain a large number of
layers, make new Layer Sets to hold them. If you want to make a new set from
existing layers, the simplest way is to link them together and then choose New
Set from Linked from the pop-up menu on the Layers palette. Remember that
you can also duplicate entire sets, which makes it easy to try out multiple
variations in your artwork.

2 Hiding and showing

THE EASIEST WAY of removing part of a layer is to delete it. But deletion is irrevocable: you can't go back later and undelete the lost elements. Using a layer mask, however, forces you into no such constraints. Areas can be hidden, using hard or soft edges, and then painted back into place if the need arises. Layer masks are one of the most powerful devices available to the photomontage artist.

Changing the way two layers interact with each other is also a vital technique to master. Layer interaction may involve altering the blending mode to allow the underlying texture to show through, or selectively hiding parts of a layer depending on its brightness values – or even depending on the brightness of the layers beneath it.

Group therapy: layer modes

1 The jacket has been separated from the figure and made into a new layer. The texture (a piece of wallpaper) is placed over the top, and completely obscures the jacket.

2 It's grouped with the jacket by pressing *Shift* *⌘* *G* *Shift* *ctrl* *G*; now, the texture is visible only where it overlaps the layer underneath.

GROUPING LAYERS together is the easiest way of constraining the visibility of one layer to that of the layer beneath.

It all gets more interesting when you start to change the mode of the grouped layer. There are more layer modes than I've shown here; I've only demonstrated the results of using some of the more interesting ones.

6 Lighten mode is similar to Screen, but with a twist: it only brightens those parts of the underlying layer that are darker than the target layer.

7 Darken mode does the opposite of Lighten. Since the background of the pattern is brighter than the suit color, it has no effect; only the relief on the pattern shows through.

3 Layer modes are changed by selecting from the pop-up menu at the top of the Layers palette. This mode is Multiply, which adds the darkness of the layer to the one beneath.

4 The opposite of Multiply is Screen: this adds the brightness of the layer to the brightness of the layer beneath, resulting in an image that's brighter than either.

5 Overlay mode is a kind of mid-point between Multiply and Screen. It's a more subtle effect than either, and allows the full texture of the jacket to show through.

8 Hard Light is a stronger version of Overlay, which increases the saturation of both layers. Some of the underlying layer's detail is often lost using Hard Light.

9 Soft Light is a toned-down version of Hard Light, producing an altogether subtler effect. The textures of the original jacket are clearly visible beneath the pattern.

10 Color Burn darkens the underlying layer, but adds a strong color element to it, producing a deeply hued result that's quite different to any of the others.

Layer masks 1: hold on tight

1 With the two elements of this simple montage placed together, we can see the problem immediately. This hand may be in the same scene as the Psion, but it isn't holding it: we need to bring the thumb to the front so that the machine appears to be gripped by it.

MOST MONTAGES involve combining objects in such a way that they interact with each other. The simplest way of putting one object 'inside' another is to use a layer mask, which allows one object to appear to be simultaneously in front of and behind another.

Layer masks have more uses than this, as we'll see later in this chapter: they're one of the most powerful weapons in the photomontage artist's arsenal, and deserve close inspection to see how you can achieve the best results from them. Here, we'll use a layer mask to place the Psion computer so it's held by the hand.

3 Using a hard-edged brush, simply paint with black over the thumb area. Because the layer is being hidden rather than erased, we can always adjust the mask to show the portions we've hidden: simply paint with white to restore the image. At the end, change the opacity back to 100%.

5 With the layer unchained from its mask, we can now move it independently and the mask will remain where it is. The object can be shifted, scaled, rotated or distorted however you choose and will still remain grasped by that thumb, because the mask now stays put.

2 One solution would be to erase the thumb area from the Psion. But that would be an irrevocable step, and would mean we couldn't move the

machine afterwards without leaving a hole. Instead, choose Layer/Add Layer Mask/Reveal All. The 'Reveal All' bit simply means that we begin with

nothing hidden. So that we can see what we're doing, it helps to lower the transparency of the Psion layer first; setting it to 50% lets us see the hand.

4 The tiny icon immediately to the left of the layer thumbnail will show either a paintbrush or a circle in a gray square, indicating whether

you're working on the layer or its mask. When the Psion is moved, the mask moves with it, as can be seen here: this is because the layer is linked to its

mask. To unlink it, click on the tiny chain icon shown between the layer thumbnail and the mask thumbnail and it will disappear.

6 Adding shadows helps the effect to look realistic. Two shadows have been added, one for the Psion and one for the hand: each shadow layer

has been grouped with its target layer, so it only shows where the two overlap. Keeping the shadows separate makes them easier to adjust later.

Layer masks 2: in the swim

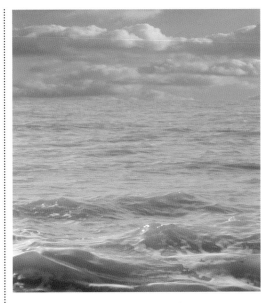

1 This sea and sky have been comped together from two different photographs. The hard line that separates them looks too rigid: this amount of cloud would surely create a hazy effect on the horizon.

PAINTING ON LAYER MASKS with black hides the layer; painting with white reveals it again. But painting with intermediate shades of gray causes the layer to become partially transparent.

Rather than choosing a gray tone, we can simulate gray by lowering the opacity of the brush tool as we paint – which is how the image of the diver's legs as seen through the water is achieved.

As well as lowering the opacity, we can also use a soft-edged rather than a hard-edged brush to paint with. This creates a fading mask, as if we'd feathered a selection and deleted it. But of course, since this is a mask, we can paint the hidden areas back in again at any time – which would be impossible if we'd chosen to delete the area instead.

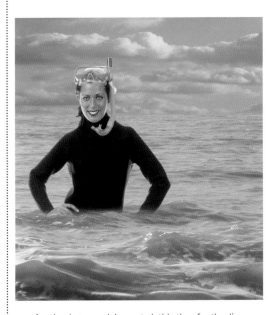

4 Another layer mask is created, this time for the diver. The bulk of her body beneath the waves is simply painted out with a large brush, to hide as much of the unwanted area as possible in one go.

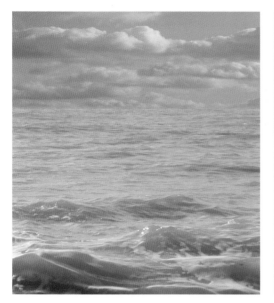

2 After creating a layer mask for the sea layer, I've simply brushed along the horizon using a small, soft-edged brush – holding the **Shift** key down to ensure a straight line as I painted. This creates the effect of a slightly feathered edge along the horizon.

3 Placing a figure in the foreground looks desperately unconvincing: the diver may occupy the same visual space as the background, but there's no sense of her fitting into it.

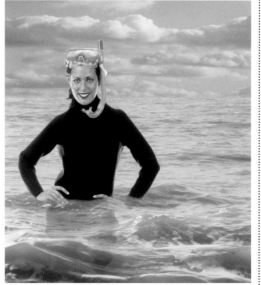

5 Switching to a much smaller, soft-edged brush, and painting with white rather than black, we can begin to paint the figure back in around the water line. By following the contours of the figure as well as those of the waves, we can make her look far more part of the scene.

6 But water is a translucent substance. Still using white, choose a larger brush and set its opacity to just 20%. By painting selectively on the mask below the water line, we can now see a hint of the diver through the sea. I've also used the Wave filter to make the diver's legs ripple slightly.

HOT TIP

When painting layer masks, you may frequently need to change brush size to create fine adjustments. Rather than picking from the pop-up list, use the keyboard shortcut: the **[** key selects a smaller brush, the **]** key selects the next larger one.

SHORTCUTS
MAC | WIN | BOTH

Layer masks 3: other tools

1 A patch of cloud has been placed directly over the top of the grass in this image. Clouds can be put to many uses in Photoshop; in this instance, we're going to turn our cloud into a rolling mist.

ANY OF THE PAINTING tools can be used on a layer mask – not just the Brush. If a tool can be used in a Photoshop layer, it can be used on the mask as well.

This greatly extends the scope of masking, as well as allowing us to create some interesting and unusual effects. Here, we'll use the Gradient tool to produce a softly feathered edge to a bank of cloud, looking just as if we'd erased it with a huge Eraser.

More interesting is the second effect, which uses the Smudge tool to create the mask by bringing in the black around the figure, so that the grass appears to overlap her convincingly.

3 This glamorous granny seems unaware of the fog rolling in behind her - but we need to make her fit into her environment better. After creating her layer mask, we first hold ⌘ *ctrl* and click on her name in the Layers palette, which loads up the area taken up by the pixels in the layer. Then inverse the selection, using ⌘ *Shift* *I* *ctrl* *Shift* *I*; fill the new selection (which includes everything except the woman) with black. You won't see any change: that comes later.

2 After creating a layer mask for the cloud layer, choose the Gradient tool and set it to Foreground to Background, using black and white as the respective foreground and background colors. Now position the Gradient tool at the bottom of the clouds and drag vertically, holding the Shift key down as you do so to create a pure vertical. The result is a smoothly fading mask: the mask itself is shown inset.

4 The layer mask we just created looks like the inset (above right). Because white is the selected area, the hidden region (black) hides nothing. Now for the interesting bit: using the Smudge tool, gradually streak up the black mask where the woman touches the ground. Each streak will hide a part of her, and the result will look as if the blades of grass are truly in front of her body. The minimal shadow, painted on a new layer behind her, simply adds to the effect.

HOT TIP

Experiment with different brushes and tools on layer masks to see the effect. Using a brush set to Dissolve, for instance, would be a good way of masking this figure if she were lying on sand rather than grass (see page 34 for an example of this technique). For less defined background surfaces, try using the Blur tool instead – set it to Darken, or it will have little effect.

SHORTCUTS
MAC | WIN | BOTH

Layer masks 4: smoothing out

CUTOUT OBJECTS CAN LOOK TOO CRISP, particularly if they've been silhouetted using the Pen tool. This hand appears false against the slightly out-of-focus background: it's an obvious montage that wouldn't fool anyone.

One technique might simply be to feather the edges of the hand. But that's an irrevocable step: anything that has been permanently deleted will be hard to put back afterwards.

A better method is to create a layer mask and adjust that, as shown here. This technique makes it easy to get exactly the amount of edge blurring you need, without having to commit yourself at any stage: you can always discard the layer mask and repeat the process with different settings later.

1 First, hold ⌘ ctrl and click on the layer name to load the selection. Make a layer mask and inverse the selection, then fill the inverted area with black. Here's how the mask looks: its crisp edges won't affect the layer yet, since it's only masked what isn't visible anyway.

4 This figure suffers from the same problem: the hard edge of that white jacket looks more like plastic than fabric, and his ear is too crisp against the background. Applying the method outlined above will rectify this situation easily.

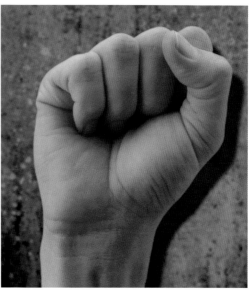

2 Now, with the inverse still selected, feather the selection by using ⌥ ⌘ D *alt* *ctrl* D and specifying the feather amount, then fill with black again. A figure of 1 or 2 pixels will be sufficient. Here's how the mask looks afterwards.

3 Now the hand looks more like it belongs with the background: the edges are softened, without a single pixel having been deleted from the layer itself. If the background changes and you need the hand to be crisp again, simply discard the mask.

5 So far, so good: the jacket and ear blend in much better with the background. The hair, however, is another matter. Because the original strands of hair were so fine, the new mask has made the individual stray hairs disappear, while the remainder now looks more like a bad wig.

6 The solution, of course, is to set the foreground color to white and simply paint out the mask around the hair edge. It's always worth checking for details like this when using this masking technique, as any fine elements can easily be lost in the process.

HOT TIP

Don't be tempted to use too high a feather amount when blurring the edges; you'll end up with an edge that looks fuzzy without being properly hidden. If you do want a large feather, then start at 2 pixels and keep repeating the process, increasing the feather amount as you go.

SHORTCUTS
MAC WIN BOTH

Blending options 1: fire power

1 Here are the two elements of this montage – the hand holding the gun, and the photograph of the firework which has been rotated to match the gun's angle. Simply changing the mode of this layer to Screen would get rid of the black, but the flame would be pale against a light background – and would become invisible against white.

THE BLENDING OPTIONS feature, tucked away within the Layer Style palette, is one of the most overlooked features in Photoshop. But it's an enormously powerful tool that allows you to hide or show picture elements automatically, without touching a brush or layer mask.

In the image above, for the Sunday Telegraph, I duplicated the background sky complete with lightning, and placed it in front of the globe; then used Blending Options to remove the sky from the front version.

3 When we zoom in on the image, however, we can see that moving the slider produces a sharp cut-off between what's visible and what's hidden. It's an ugly, stepping effect; in order to make the effect more realistic, we need to look more closely at exactly how that black slider operates.

5 Further adjustment of both sliders allows us to set the visibility of this layer exactly as we want it. Now, the left slider is set to 50 and the right slider to 120, which removes exactly the right amount of black without weakening the effect of the rather enthusiastic gunshot.

2 Double-click the layer's name or choose Layer/Layer Style/Blending Options to bring up the dialog. It's the bottom section we want to look at, the one headed Blend If. On the This Layer

section, drag the black triangle to the right – here, it's at a position of 10 (working on a scale of 0=black to 255=white). This hides everything darker than 10 in the image.

4 What appears to be a single triangle is, in fact, two. Hold down ⌥ *alt* as you drag and it will split into its two sections, which can be

manipulated individually. With the left slider still set to 10, we now drag the right one out to a position of 75. This is what happens: everything darker than

10 is hidden, and everything brighter than 75 is fully visible. But now, all the values in between fade smoothly between the two states.

6 When placed against a suitable background (somehow libraries always come to mind when I think of gunshots) the effect is dramatic. I don't

believe there's any other way that this flame could have been isolated from its background as convincingly as this in Photoshop.

Blending options 2: plane view

THIS SECTION DEALS WITH the other half of the Blending Options dialog – the Underlying Layer section. This controls the visibility of the target layer depending on all the layers beneath it, not just the one directly below.

The illustration above was for a Sunday Times Magazine cover, illustrating the crowded state of Britain's air traffic. Rather than creating an Underlying Layer adjustment for each plane, I duplicated the cloud layer to the front and removed the blue sky from that layer: seen through it were not only the planes, but the original sky as well.

1 In this example, we're going to make the plane fly through the clouds rather than just sitting on top. Working on the plane layer, it's clear that we don't want to hide that layer depending on its brightness values: unlike the example on the previous page, this isn't simply a case of removing the black element from the target layer.

3 Since we're working with blending values rather than with a layer mask, we can move the plane anywhere we want within the artwork and the effect will still apply. This is a great technique for animation, and works well if you're planning to import Photoshop artwork into After Effects.

2 Because we want the visibility of the plane to be affected by the presence of cloud in the layer beneath, we need to turn our attention away from the This Layer section of the

Blending Options dialog, and look instead at the Underlying Layer section. This works in exactly the same way, except – as its name implies – the visibility of the target layer is

determined by what's going on underneath. Here, we've dragged and split the right (white) slider rather than the left (black) one; settings of 118 and 167 do the job well.

Not all clouds are as obliging as these. If the gray values in the cloud are the same as those in the sky, you'll need to add a layer mask as well, painting out the offending areas by hand.

4 Although we hid the plane in the clouds correctly, the overall effect can be made more realistic by allowing a little of the plane to show through –

after all, clouds are not solid objects. This is achieved by dragging the right slider back towards the right, increasing the number: in this instance,

a value of 196 as the white cutoff point is enough to add just a touch of translucence to what would otherwise be over-opaque clouds.

39

Graphics tablets

I SPENT SEVERAL YEARS reviewing graphics tablets for MacUser, praising their capabilities and deriding their shortcomings, while all the time secretly wondering why anyone would use such an awkward device. When each new tablet arrived I'd expect a liberating feeling, hoping that I could finally discard my mouse and sketch as if I was drawing on paper with a pencil. And each time I felt frustrated, because drawing on a tablet while looking up at a monitor is nothing like drawing on paper. And then I realized the problem.

Graphics tablets take a lot of getting used to.

Using a stylus is very different to using a mouse. For one thing, it isn't tied to your computer, which means it can roll around the desk, drop into the waste paper basket and have to be rescued from among a pile of junk mail before it ends up as landfill. The stylus could end up anywhere: at least a mouse can't be more than a cord's length away.

My main problem with the stylus, though, was that although it seemed perfectly adequate for shading and painting, it was too clumsy for drawing Pen paths and laughable for web browsing. There's also the problem that while a mouse moves the cursor in the direction you choose – and you can site a mouse anywhere on the mouse pad while you drag it around – the stylus and tablet have a one-to-one relationship with the monitor: the top left corner of the tablet represents the top left corner of the screen. You can't simply position a stylus anywhere you want it and expect it to behave like a mouse.

In theory, I could have used the mouse for some tasks, and the stylus and tablet for others. But the mouse wouldn't work properly on the tablet's surface, and in order to use the tablet I had to place it on top of my mouse mat and then take it away again to use the mouse. So the tablet always ended up sitting on the shelf until the PR agency who'd lent it to me sent out a courier to pick it up again.

Then I was sent a combined mouse/stylus combination to review. Made by Wacom, it's the cheapest tablet they produce: at a cost of under $100, I fully expected it to be more of a toy than the kind of tool a serious graphic artist would give a second glance.

The first thing that surprised me was the mouse. It was cordless, which felt decidedly modern. True, it was no longer chained to my computer, but at least it couldn't roll off the desk like the stylus. There was no ball to clog up, which meant the regular task of scrubbing my mouse ball and scraping the rollers with a fingernail were finally a thing of the past.

The mouse also had two buttons, which was quite a novelty for a diehard Mac user, although I spent many hours trying to decide what to do with the second button (you can customize it to do anything you like, and even change its function depending on the application you're working in). But best of all, the mouse had a scroll wheel that let me zip through web pages, tear down Word documents and whizz through image libraries without having to click on one of those annoyingly small arrow icons at the corners of windows.

I started using the mouse in earnest, glancing occasionally at the stylus as it perched in its holder at the top of the tablet. Once in a while I'd reach for the stylus when I wanted to perform a task for which variable pressure would be useful, such as painting shadows or using the Dodge and Burn tools.

Gradually, over the weeks, I began to feel more at home with the stylus, and found myself using it increasingly often. Now I find that I'd be lost without it: I take it with me everywhere I take my PowerBook, and if I ever have to give a demonstration where I have to use the mouse that comes with the demo computer, it feels clumsy and awkward.

The upshot of all this is that I now recommend a graphics tablet wholeheartedly to anyone who'll listen, to the extent that I consider them an essential tool.

Just don't expect to take to it immediately.

3 Composing the scene

COMPOSITION, as any art historian will tell us, makes the difference between a good picture and a bad one. So it is with photomontage: the position of people and objects within the montage enables us to tell the story we want to tell. As we'll see in the first few examples in this chapter, the relative positions of characters can completely change the message we're putting across.

One way of making a montage look more realistic is to place our characters so that they interact with their background. Films which use a lot of computer-generated imagery, such as Jurassic Park, always go to great lengths to show their subjects part-hidden by foliage and other foreground elements: it's this incorporation within the picture that makes them more convincing.

Location is everything

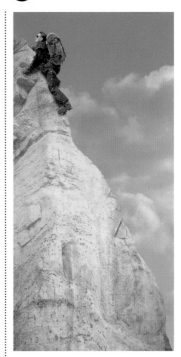

1 With the climber positioned right at the top, we can see how far he's climbed. Our view of the mountain shows the task that he's accomplished to date; but we have no way of telling whether he's just started out, or if he's nearing completion. The rest of the climb may be visible to him, but the viewer is left with no sense of the job that awaits him.

THE WAY AN IMAGE IS CROPPED can have dramatic results in terms of the story being told. Here, we're looking at a montage in which the mountain, the climber and the sky are three separate elements that can be rearranged as we choose; but the same principles apply to cropping an existing image. The fact that this image is composed of three layers simply makes it easier for us to arrange the elements to tell the climber's story as we see it.

As it stands, the image above left shows a mountain climber on a piece of rock. Placed bang in the middle of the frame, the positioning tells us almost nothing about his progress: it's a static picture in which the climber is fixed in place, moving neither up nor down. The strong diagonal of the mountainside,

2 Moving the climber to the bottom has the opposite effect. Now we get a good idea of the task in front of the climber, as we can see how far he still has to go. The presence of all that sky, though, positions him some distance up the slope.

3 When we move the mountain down so that the majority of the image is taken up with sky, we get a much stronger impression of the climber nearing the peak. With so much sky around him, we can share his sense of isolation and solitude. All this sky shows us that there isn't another person around for miles.

4 By moving the mountain so that it takes up most of the frame, we position it so that our own viewpoint interacts with the picture. Where before the focus was on the climber, now the viewer can get a sense of the hardship faced. So much rock face highlights the climber's daunting task.

HOT TIP

To make the climber appear to climb the mountain, a shadow has been added beneath him. This shadow was created on a separate layer, and grouped with the mountainside so that it is only visible where it overlaps the mountain; at the same time, it was linked to the climber so that it moved with him as his position was adjusted.

running from top left to bottom right, divides the image neatly in two as it delineates the difference between the land and the sky; but that neatness also takes away all sense of the dramatic.

Cropping a picture enables the viewer to focus on the key image without being distracted by extraneous elements. But it also allows the picture editor, or the digital artist, to tell the story they want to tell rather than simply reproducing the scene as it originally appeared.

While the use of photomontage in newspapers has attracted much criticism amid claims of it distorting the truth, few readers complain about the way images are cropped – and yet the story is determined as much by cropping as by montage.

45

Relative values: interaction

1 Simply moving them closer together so that they overlap helps to establish a link between them. By flipping the girl horizontally, both figures are now angled towards the centre of the image.

5 Now the tables have been turned. It's the daughter who is in the dominant position, while the father remains distanced from her: like most parents, he's now concerned that she's moving away from him.

COMBINING TWO PEOPLE in a montage entails more than just placing them on the same background. You've got to work out the relationship between them, and position them to tell the story in the best way. The image above shows, let's say, a father and daughter. They may share the same space but the reader gets no hint of how they might interact; by varying their position we can make their relationship clear.

2 A simple additional device such as the hand on her shoulder puts the father in a more protective role. His attitude is one of pride with, perhaps, a hint of restraint.

3 Bringing the father to the front still establishes his protectiveness, but now there's a sense that the safeguard is needed: he's shielding her from the viewer, while she is content to take refuge behind him.

4 By moving her towards the back we create an emotional as well as physical distance between them. Flipping her so that her shoulders point away from his accentuates the disparity: she now resents his control.

6 When we tuck the father behind the daughter, we strengthen the sense of her supremacy over him. In the previous example, she was merely moving away; now she's beginning to eclipse him.

7 Flipping the father horizontally makes him face away from his daughter metaphorically. His understanding of her is less than in the last example, but her pose shows she's prepared to turn back to him.

8 Flipping the daughter alters her body language as well: the two figures are now opposed, their shoulders pointing in different directions as she now turns her back on him absolutely.

I only have eyes for you

1 With both characters gazing directly at us, there's no contact between them – and we're left with no idea what either of them is thinking.

ON THE PREVIOUS PAGE, WE LOOKED at how changing body position can make a difference to the apparent relationship between people in a montage. But body language is only one way of explaining a relationship: far more subtle – and just as effective – is eye contact.

The photomontage artist often has to work with mugshots of politicians and celebrities, or images from a royalty-free collection. Either way, you're more or less guaranteed that the subjects will be gazing straight at the camera, and probably grinning inanely at the same time. This may suit the needs of the celebrity's publicist, but it's of little help when combining two or more people within a scene.

Here, we've taken a glamorous couple – so glamorous that he's just won an Oscar – and moved their eyes around from frame to frame. Nothing else has been changed, and yet the entire expression alters with the position of the eyes. The nine examples here are just a small part of the infinite range of expressions that can be achieved by simply changing the eyes.

4 He now looks a little over protective of his trophy, as if someone might be about to snatch it from him: but she's downcast, as if the prize should have been hers.

7 He now gazes excitedly into the future – who knows what doors this prize will open? She isn't so much annoyed with him as just plain bored by the whole evening.

2 He's looking at her hopefully, and the grin has become almost a leer. Her reply is ambiguous, but not wholly negative – she might go along with his plans, she might not.

3 His expression hasn't changed, but hers certainly has. No chance for him tonight: she's fed up with the whole idea and can't wait to be rid of him.

5 Now he's gazing up at his adoring audience – a subtle difference from the previous example. She, however, only has eyes for the trophy.

6 Now he's really worried, glancing over his shoulder as if he expects to be mugged - and that grin looks more false than ever. Her mind is somewhere else entirely.

8 He stares in wonder at his trophy as if he can't believe he's really won it. She ponders the situation, wondering if next time the accolade will go to her instead.

9 Now he's thanking heaven for the prize which has been awarded him – whereas she is wondering if she just saw a mouse scuttle across the floor.

HOT TIP

To change the direction a character's eyes are looking in, you need to create two new layers – one for the eyeball, and one for the pupil: group the pupil with the eyeball, and you can move it around within the eye. For more about working with eyes, see Chapter 5, Heads and Bodies.

The politics of plurality

1 The supplied mugshots of Prescott and Mowlam. The original bodies were useless, so were deleted.

2 This body, taken from a royalty-free collection, had the right kind of dynamic pose – with the benefit of one hand being raised, which is perfect for holding a mask aloft. Mo Mowlam's head has simply been placed on top to make sure it would fit.

THIS ILLUSTRATION WAS COMMISSIONED to accompany an article in the Daily Telegraph about how politicians spot themselves in coded form in works of fiction. Only two politicians were mentioned directly in the article – Deputy Prime Minister John Prescott, and former Northern Ireland Secretary Mo Mowlam. The idea of using masks came from the editor, to show the 'real' politicians being revealed beneath the thin disguises.

When compiling an image with several elements, it's important to draw the reader's eye: this is accomplished using the strong diagonal of the masks and faces, reinforced by the angles of the fence and buildings.

6 By placing Prescott's body behind Mowlam's, I got around the fact that his hand didn't join his arm. Moving Mowlam's eyes creates reader engagement; erasing her left arm made the two bodies fit together better.

3 Masking Mowlam's neck made the head fit the body perfectly. A new hand was needed to hold the mask – a mock-glamor mask chosen to neatly counterpoint Mowlam's evident lack of glamor.

4 Because Mowlam's body is so animated, I wanted a more passive pose for Prescott to counter it. This casual shirt was all wrong, as was the fact that he didn't have a spare hand; but these were problems that could be sorted out later.

5 Prescott's new shirt was pasted inside the shirt area on the original jacket. The hand was slotted into a section of sleeve made by copying an existing sleeve portion. (The less said about the elbow problem, the better.)

HOT TIP

Fitting heads onto bodies is more than just a question of finding two images taken from the same angle: you need to match the colors and shading of the two so that they blend together well. To find out more about how to do this, see Chapter 5, Heads and Bodies.

7 The image of the Houses of Parliament affirms that these figures are politicians. I took this photograph ensuring that the railings in the foreground would frame whatever I put in front of them.

8 The new sky adds interest to the original overcast image. Two more 'politicians' have been added on the right; placing them behind the railings puts them firmly in the scene, as we'll see on the following pages.

Back to the foreground

1 When the farmer is pasted on top of the background, he looks like he doesn't belong there. Well, he doesn't – this patch of grass is really waste ground in the middle of a road junction. To make the scene work more convincingly, we need to make the farmer become part of the background rather than simply standing in front of it as he does at the moment.

PLACING PEOPLE within a scene is rarely a matter of sticking them on top – because they rarely look like they belong there. To make the image more convincing, the people need to interact with the background to some degree. The easiest way to do this is to take a background element and bring it to the front: it's often a simple task, but it makes all the difference, as we'll see with this illustration of an urban farmer swamped by his modern-day environment.

4 With the pitchfork now in front of the fence, which in turn is in front of the farmer, he looks fully integrated into the scene. A shadow of the pitchfork is painted on the fence, and another shadow created beneath the farmer; finally, small wisps are masked around his feet to make it look like blades of grass are growing up in front of them.

2 The fence is made up of straight lines, so it's a simple matter to select the front half of it using the Pen tool, make a new layer and bring it to the front. If you really can't get on with the Pen tool, use the Lasso instead – hold down ⌥ *alt* to constrain the tool to creating straight lines between pairs of click points. Now, the farmer is far more integrated.

3 This is a simple trick: I just selected the bottom half of his pitchfork, made a new layer out of it using ⌘ *J* *ctrl* *J* and brought it to the front.

5 The background in the original image is busy, as befits an urban road system - but so busy that it's distracting attention. So the top half of the background was selected and blurred using Gaussian Blur, to knock it slightly out of focus. To make the fence section fit, the left edge of that layer was also blurred to blend into the background.

HOT TIP

The final step requires that the background be selectively blurred - more at the back, less at the front. Go into QuickMask mode and, using the Gradient tool set to black-white, drag from top to bottom. This creates an area that's 100% selected at the top and 0% selected at the bottom: when you exit QuickMask and apply the blur, the image will be affected more at the top than at the bottom.

SHORTCUTS
MAC WIN BOTH

Playing with perspective

RELATIVE SIZE is a commodity that you can use to your advantage when composing montages. In this example, the product is the star – in this case, it's the PDA that needs to be the prominent object in the final composition. The background figure of the man holding the device is there to provide visual interest: adding him into the mix prevents the final illustration from looking like a mere product shot. As is so often the case, it's the human element that draws the reader in to the picture.

1 Simply placing the PDA in the man's hand accomplishes the task to a degree, but the tiny size of the device when included at actual size makes it too insignificant; it's barely visible in the mix.

It might be possible to create this image using just a hand, rather than the whole person. But when working with cutout objects, which always enliven a layout, it's important to ensure that the whole image is shown. Cutting off an arm at the wrist, or fading it away to white, is a poor solution: cut-off elements destroy the cutout's power, and are always a poor compromise.

IMAGE: STOCKBYTE

2 By enlarging the PDA to a ludicrously large size (above), it is brought clearly to the foreground. But we still need to show the 'actual size' of the machine; it is, after all, a pocket-sized device, and simply enlarging it would give the reader a false sense of its scale. Adding the hand at the same scale reaffirms the size of the PDA as a hand-held object, and the figure now looks as if he's holding it out towards us. The shadow painted on the PDA makes it appear as if it's being held by the hand.

3 If this composition were a single photograph, an accomplished photographer might be able to devise a means by which both the foreground object and the man in the background were both in focus – although, given the extreme difference in the apparent nearness of the two elements, it would be a daunting task.

For the purposes of convincing montage, we can take the opposite approach: adding a small degree of Gaussian Blur to the background figure (right) accentuates the sense of perspective, and forces the reader's attention onto the PDA. Blurred images are hard to focus on, by definition; adding a degree of blur allows us to direct the reader to the areas of the image we want to highlight.

HOT TIP

The hand used in step 3 here is the same one I used on the daughter's shoulder in the section Relative Values, earlier in this chapter. The hands in original photographs are rarely in the right position for a convincing montage: with a digital camera, it's easy to build up a library of suitable hand poses.

The view from the top

1 A section of wall is duplicated until it's large enough to fill the space, and then distorted to fit the perspective of the figure. Use `⌘` `T` `ctrl` `T` to enter Free Transform, then hold `⌥` `Shift` `⌘` `alt` `Shift` `ctrl` as you drag a corner handle to create the perspective transformation.

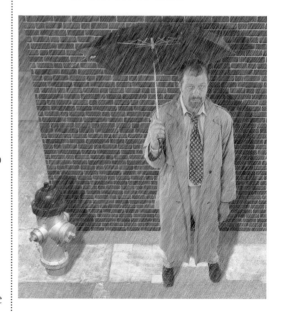

PHOTO LIBRARIES HAVE RECENTLY taken to including a large number of this kind of 'up the ladder' shot, to fit in with the current vogue for more in-your-face imagery. In most cases, shots like this are almost impossible to use in a standard montage; but moving the viewpoint of the entire scene from head-on to overhead can create an image that's much more striking and evocative.

Here, we'll look at some simple ways to create a convincing background that will make this kind of image work.

4 The rain is added by creating a new layer and filling it with white, then applying a large amount of Gaussian Noise. This noise then has Motion Blur applied to it to turn the noise into streaks, and the layer mode is set to Hard Light to allow the scene beneath to become visible through it.

2 The pavement is added in much the same way as the wall. The fire hydrant simply provides a visual counter to the umbrella man, and makes a reference to the water that will besiege him.

3 A base is added to the wall by taking a section of the front of the pavement and coloring and distorting it to fit. The shadows of the man and the hydrant help to position them within the scene.

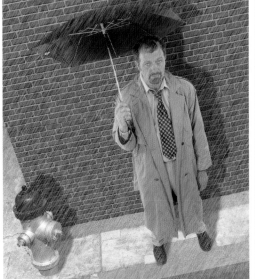

5 The rain is masked slightly over the man's face and front, and under the umbrella, to make it less distracting. Finally, the saturation of the wall is reduced significantly: the original wall was photographed on a sunny day, and the colors were too bright for this amount of rain.

6 It would have been possible to stop there. But the image was too rectilinear and static: by rotating the entire artwork we turn it into a far more dramatic and striking illustration. Note that a strip of curbstone has had to be created at the bottom, where the pavement ended.

HOT TIP

When composing images using a strong perspective such as this, remember that the position of each object within the scene will affect its perspective view. The fire hydrant, for example, has had to be distorted so that it slants to the left in order to make it visually correct.

SHORTCUTS
MAC WIN BOTH

An object lesson

WHEN WORKING with images from a range of sources, the trick is to make them all look as if they belong in the same space. This montage, commissioned by .net magazine, was to accompany an article about online auctions – dealing with the value of the stuff you might find lying around in your attic.

All the elements were photographed separately (the originals are shown along the bottom of this page), and needed to be combined in a convincing manner.

Relative sizes are important in a montage such as this, which needed to look as realistic as possible.

1 The perspective on the mug didn't match that of the rest of the artwork. The solution was simple: an elliptical selection was made of the top of the mug, which was then stretched vertically until it looked right.

2 The toy car wasn't included in the original photographs – but a three-dimensional object was needed to round off the top of the video stack and to bring the height closer to that of the Action Man.

4 Because the illustration was going right across a double page spread, I had to be careful to ensure that none of the important elements were divided by the gutter (the gap between the pages). The blank space above the monkey was left for the headline.

5 The monkey's fur was cut out using the Magic Eraser tool, which did a good job of removing all the white background while preserving the detail.

6 The soldier was originally facing left to right, as if he was running off the spread. But by flipping him horizontally he was made to face into the illustration rather than out of it, drawing the reader's eye back into the page.

7 Before the shadows were added, the montage looked flat and inauthentic. As ever, it's the use of light and shade that makes a montage come to life.

Painting shadows directly on the objects would have caused problems if I needed to move them later. Instead, I created a new shadow layer and, for each object, loaded the object's outline as a selection by ⌘ ctrl clicking on the object's name in the Layers palette, and then removed the outline of any objects on top of it by ⌥ ⌘ alt ctrl clicking on their names. That way, all the shadows could be created on a single, editable layer.

3 The records, comics and stickerbook were all photographed directly from above. By distorting each image using Free Transform, it was possible to arrange them so that they appeared to be lying on the surface.

SHORTCUTS
MAC WIN BOTH

Montage in three dimensions

1 Three photographs of chairs provide the perspective view I want (the chair on the left has been duplicated and distorted slightly). It's now just a matter of arranging the chairs so that they look convincing in their position.

CREATING A THREE-DIMENSIONAL SCENE from scratch means paying close attention to perspective; often, it involves working from given objects and making the rest of the scene match that perspective.

This illustration for the Independent on Sunday was for an article about backbiting gossip in the parliamentary tea room of the House of Commons. The trouble was, the newspaper held no photographs of the tea room; but eye-witness reports described the wood paneling, the type of wallpaper and the green leather color scheme.

The photographs of the chairs came from the Hemera photo library, which frequently includes shots of the same object from several different angles. These provided the base perspective; the walls, floor and other elements were drawn to match it.

4 The wood panels are duplicated, flipped horizontally and darkened slightly – these will be beneath the window, so will have less light on them. We've now built the corner of our room, and the remaining elements can be added.

7 Populating the scene is simply a matter of sticking the relevant politicians' heads onto bodies that could sit and stand in the correct way. The seated figures have been masked where they overlap the chairs, so it looks as if they're sitting in them.

2 A scan of a piece of wood is shaded to give the impression of paneling, and then duplicated to make a row of wooden panels. It looks wholly artificial seen in isolation, but makes more sense when included in the main scene.

3 The row of paneling is placed behind all the chairs, and distorted using Free Transform to follow the perspective of the backs of the chairs. Since two chairs were placed right against the wall, it's fairly easy to match their perspective with some accuracy,

5 A scan of a small section of wallpaper is duplicated, colored to match the green/gold color scheme and distorted to fit the perspective set by the panels. The carpet is drawn by filling a green rectangle with Gaussian Noise; the skirting, dado and picture rails are shaded wooden strips.

6 The door and window have been distorted, again using Free Transform, to match the set perspective. The view outside the window is a photograph of the House of Commons itself – fortunately the building is built around a courtyard, which makes sense of the view!

8 The props – the glasses, teacups, table and monitor showing the debating chamber – help to make sense of the scene as a whole. The monitor also gives John Major, seen on his phone at the back, a reason for turning his head to the side.

9 The final task is to add shadows to make the objects sit more comfortably in the space. A shadow layer is placed above the floor, walls and paneling to add general shading; additional shadow layers grouped with the chairs help to make the politicians sit down.

Digital cameras

A DIGITAL CAMERA is an essential tool for the Photoshop artist. They've gone from being interesting toys to must-have tools in the space of a few years, and every year or so a new model appears that redefines the field. Having reviewed many cameras for MacUser, I've found myself frequently having to buy the latest model since, after playing with it for a couple of weeks, I've been unable to send it back. I'm now on my fifth camera, and each one has been a significant improvement on the one it replaced.

There are several issues to consider when buying a camera. Image quality is of major importance, and a lot depends on the quality of the lens. Equipment from traditional camera manufacturers such as Kodak, Nikon and Canon tends to be better than that from the electronics giants, simply because they have more experience in making good lenses.

One factor which determines image quality is the amount of compression used to fit the images into the camera's memory. Images are compressed using the JPEG format: the smaller the size the image is squeezed into, the poorer the quality. This 'lossiness', as it's known, manifests itself in a certain blockiness to the pixels seen in large areas of flat color, and in stray pixels of the wrong color, known as artifacts. Better cameras will allow you to choose the level of compression as well as the size of the image; some allow you to save images as uncompressed TIFF files, which take up a lot of memory (around five times the best JPEG quality) but will result in the cleanest image.

The chief consideration when buying a camera is the size of the images it captures, measured in pixels. For comparison, cameras are sold according to their image size in millions of pixels, or megapixels for short. A typical mid-range camera will deliver images of around 3.3 megapixels, which equates to a Photoshop image measuring 2048 x 1536 pixels (proportions are always in the ratio of 4:3, matching the aspect ratio of most computer monitors). In practical terms, this means that you can use the images up to a size of around 10 x 7.5 inches if used at 200 dpi, or around 6.8 x 5 inches if used at the best resolution of 300 dpi. Which, in rough terms, means that you can use the image in print at around half magazine page size at top quality, or nearly full page size if you're not so fussy. The newer mid-range cameras now boast a resolution of 5 megapixels, with a corresponding increase in the size an image can be printed.

In general, the digital artist won't be capturing images to be used at anything like this size. I use my camera to photograph the sort of things I don't have on royalty-free CDs: bathroom sinks, telephone boxes, swivel chairs and all the other objects which are easy to locate but hard to find pictures of. Most importantly, I use my camera to photograph myself: in my montages I've been the torso of both George W Bush and Al Gore, the body of Prince Philip, and the hands of celebrities from Mick Jagger to Albert Einstein.

Which brings me to my final requirement: an LCD viewing screen that can swivel so it faces in the same direction as the lens. This is a feature not found on all cameras, probably because it's a somewhat esoteric requirement: but when I'm standing with my arms raised in anger wearing a black bow tie while wielding an Oscar, I need to see what's going on before the timer counts down to take the picture. It's for this reason that I've tended to choose cameras from the Nikon Coolpix range, which combine the swivel feature with excellent image quality. The Coolpix 5000, shown here, is my current camera; retailing at around $1000, it has a resolution of 5 megapixels and takes top-quality pictures.

One final suggestion: always carry your camera with you when you go out. You never know when you'll stumble across a rare object, a good texture or an unusual building – or even the back of an interesting head.

4 Light and shade

SHADOWS ARE THE KEY to placing people and objects within the scene. Without shadows, images can look dull and unconvincing; even the hint of a shadow can make a montage come to life. First, we'll look at some of the ways of creating and using shadows to your advantage.

Light is another matter. Whether it's the beam from a table lamp or the glow around a candle, or the suggestion of sunlight across a scene, visible light can add interest and mystery to a montage. It's easier to create than you might think, although such elements as the flame of a candle can take a little effort to get right.

We'll also look at how to make a neon sign that looks like the real thing, and how to simulate an image on a screen.

Shadows on the ground

1 Duplicate the figure layer, lock the transparency (using the checkbox on the Layers palette, or the shortcut ⌀) and fill the layer with black – use ⌥ Delete alt Delete to fill with the foreground color.

GROUND SHADOWS are among the easiest types of shadow to create in Photoshop. To make them convincing, you'll need to put in a small amount of extra effort: here, we'll look at how to graduate the blurring effect so that the shadow appears to lie in a true perspective plane as it fades away from the viewer, rather than just darkening the background.

Creating shadows directly from existing objects is always easier than trying to paint them to match. They're also more convincing, as they correspond precisely to the object or person being shadowed.

5 The shadow needs to be more blurred at the back to look convincing. But simply blurring the whole shadow, as shown here, makes it far too indistinct at the front, and the man looks like he's floating.

2 Now uncheck the Lock Transparency box (or use ☑ again) and then use Free Transform to distort the shadow so that it lies along the ground.

3 The bottom of the shadow, where it meets the object, almost certainly won't conform to it – so just use the Eraser and the Brush tool to paint it where it should go.

4 The shadow will need some softening so it doesn't look too harsh. Use Gaussian Blur to add a small degree of blurring: here, a radius of 2 pixels has been applied.

6 The solution is to go into QuickMask mode (press **Q**) and then use the Gradient tool to drag from the top of the shadow (not the top of the image) to the bottom. This will create a graduated selection.

7 Now, when you exit QuickMask (use **Q** again), the shadow will be fully selected at the top, and not selected at the bottom. Apply a Gaussian Blur again (8 pixels used here) to see the graduated blurring effect.

8 To make the shadow fade away, make a layer mask for the shadow layer and use the Gradient tool once again, dragging from top to bottom. The higher you start, the more opaque the top of the shadow will be.

HOT TIP

If you're using a layer mask to selectively fade the shadow, as detailed in the final step here, you could spend hours with the Gradient tool trying to get the fade just right. But there's an easier way: after the first application of the tool, you can use Brightness and Contrast on the layer mask to change its balance and opacity – and it will work without changing the underlying layer.

SHORTCUTS
MAC | WIN | BOTH

Shadows on the wall

IMAGE: STOCKBYTE

1 To create the shadow, duplicate the layer and fill it with black in the same manner as shown on the previous page.

SHADOWS ON WALLS are also easy to create – but you have to think about the relationship between the figure and the surface the shadow is cast upon. The closer the shadow is to the figure, the closer the figure will appear to be to the wall.

Under normal lighting conditions, the shadow will be placed slightly below the figure to give the impression of natural daylight illumination. But raised shadows can have a different effect: the immediate impression is to make the figure look more sinister, as if lit from below (which is why the baddies in horror movies often carry candles just below their faces).

The illustration above was commissioned by the newspaper Sunday Business to illustrate how world leaders were shuffling money around the globe via the International Monetary Fund. Placing the shadows on the wall above them heightened the sense of their power, as well as reinforcing the light source – the illuminated map around which they're gathered. Of course, a real illuminated table would never cast shadows as crisp as this one, but it's the overall impression that's more important to the image than optical accuracy.

5 When the shadow is enlarged, the light source looks closer to the figure: when it's raised up, the light source is low down, making the figure look more sinister.

2 Because the surface is flat, an even blur can be applied to the whole shadow. Reducing the transparency of the layer allows the wall to show through behind it.

3 Moving the shadow closer to the figure positions him closer to the wall: here, he's standing with his shoulder almost leaning against the surface.

4 Darkening the wall itself helps to make the shadow look real. A simple black-to-transparent graduation created on a new layer makes the wall look more convincing.

6 With a light source this close, we need some shading on the figure itself. This shadow is simply painted on a new layer, which is grouped with the figure layer so it only intersects it.

7 When the background shows the ground as well as a wall, we need to combine both shadow techniques detailed so far: the shadow must run along the ground, then up the wall.

8 Easily done: the shadow is offset, then the bottom (where it overlaps the wall) is distorted to join the feet. Some extra painting and erasing is needed to complete the effect.

HOT TIP

Create shadows on their own layer, filling them with solid black. Then reduce the transparency of the whole layer until you get the effect you want. This is far more reliable than filling the layer with a low opacity first, as it's easier to change when the illustration is complete.

Shadows that focus the action

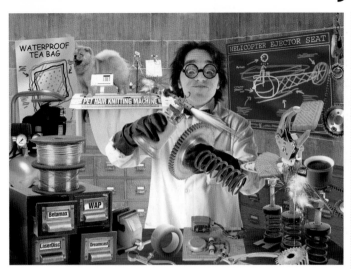

THIS COMPLEX MONTAGE, created for the magazine Computer Active, was to illustrate scientific inventions that didn't quite make the grade. In addition to the real life failures, shown on the file drawers at the front (Betamax, WAP phones, LaserDiscs and Dreamcast) there are also more fanciful technologies – such as the pet hair knitting machine, the self-dunking biscuit, and the helicopter ejector seat.

The illustration needed to have a lot of elements to portray the chaos of the inventive laboratory: but with so much going on, the completed montage (above) was too confusing on the eye. By adding a range of shadows and lighting effects, the finished image (at the bottom of the facing page) enabled the reader to focus on the scientist figure without distraction. All the other elements were still there for perusal, but reader was no longer assailed by a mass of visual data. Shadows, as shown here, have the ability to focus the eye.

1 In this montage there's a very clear light source – the blowtorch in the scientist's hand. To make this focal point come to life, we need to add not only shading behind it, but a glow from it. A new layer was set to Hard Light mode and grouped with the scientist, so it would only show up where it intersected him.

4 A new layer was created just below the table layer (there were 49 layers in total in the completed montage) to add shading to the background. Using a large, soft brush (400 pixels) and black paint, set on an opacity of 30%, shading was added to the extremities of the image – around the sides and corners, where the light from the blowtorch would not reach. Extra shading was also painted in directly behind the edge of the table, to bring it forward and add a sense of depth to the illustration.

2 Hard Light allows both shadows and light to be painted on in a translucent manner: so the back of his head was painted with black, and the front with an orange hue sampled from the blowtorch flame itself. Setting the brush tool to a low opacity made it easier to build up the effect in slow stages.

3 With the shading and glare on the scientist in place, it was a simple matter to position the shadow of the scientist on the wall behind. The shadow would be made by the blowtorch, so it was enlarged and positioned so that it appeared to be cast from this source.

5 Next, a new layer was created right at the top of the montage, to add shading to the foreground objects. Being at the front, they would tend to jump out at the viewer; since the intended focus was in the mid-ground, the shading was necessary to distract attention from the foreground. The information here was important, since it included the filing cabinet labels that held the key to the whole montage; but these were details that the reader could spot later.

6 The final shadow was that of the dog and knitting machine cast on the wall behind it – again using the blowtorch as the light source. Since the dog was closer to the wall than the scientist, its shadow was correspondingly less blurred. The finished montage contained exactly the same elements as it did before the shadows were added, but now the reader had the chance to take in the key points before reading the information in the rest of the illustration.

Multiple shadowed objects

1 This photograph of a playing card has been distorted using Free Transform to make it appear as if it's lying on a horizontal surface.

THROUGHOUT THIS CHAPTER I've recommended always creating shadows on a separate layer. But there are times when a shadow should be part of the layer to which it belongs, as in the example shown here.

It would have been possible to create this stack of cards using a separate layer for each card, and then simply flattening all the layers at the end. But since a pack like this could include up to 52 layers (54 if you include jokers), we'd be talking about a document that's unnecessarily unwieldy for the effect we're trying to create. This way, we can draw an entire pack of cards in a single layer.

The technique used to get rid of the overhanging shadows in steps 9 to 11 is a little tricky. Here's how it works: when we go into QuickMask mode, the solid cards are shown as solid red; the partly transparent shadows are a paler pink. Using the Levels control, we can work on the mask as if it were a normal layer. So we adjust the mask so that the pale pink disappears, leaving just the solid red – the fully selected area. When we then exit QuickMask, our selection will be constrained to just the area that was fully opaque initially, so inversing and deleting the rest will get rid of the unwanted shadows.

4 Select the card pixels again. Then use ⌥⌘D *alt ctrl D* to feather the selection: with the Marquee tool selected, nudge the selection area down a couple of pixels, set the foreground color to black, and use Fill (Edit menu) to fill *behind* at an opacity of 50%.

7 Any number of cards can be stacked up in this way: as long as you keep the ⌥ *alt* key held down, you'll keep moving copies. Don't make the offsets too regular!

10 Now we can 'tighten up' that shadow using the Levels control. Drag the white arrow slider to the right, and the partly selected (lighter red) area will vanish.

2 The first step is to give some depth to the card. Begin by 'loading up' the pixels in its layer – hold `⌘` `ctrl` and click on the name in the Layers palette.

3 Now hold `⌥` `alt` and nudge the card up a couple of pixels: then inverse the selection using `Shift` `⌘` `I` `Shift` `ctrl` `I` and darken up the edge you've just created.

5 This creates a soft shadow beneath the card – but on the same layer as the card. Make a duplicate of this layer to work on, as we'll need the original later.

6 Now Select All using `⌘` `A` `ctrl` `A`. Holding down the `⌥` `alt` key with the Move tool selected, move the card to create a copy on top – and the shadow moves with it.

8 But there's a problem here: if we zoom in, we can see that there are shadows beneath the overhang of the cards where there's nothing for them to sit on.

9 To get rid of the excess shadows, select the card layers by `⌘` `ctrl` clicking on the layer name, and go into QuickMask mode by pressing `Q`.

11 All we need to do now is to exit QuickMask and inverse the selection, then press Delete: those extraneous shadows will simply disappear.

12 The last step is to bring back that original card that we duplicated, so we return the shadow beneath the bottom card in the stack.

HOT TIP

The nudge keys will behave differently depending on which tool is currently active. If the Move tool is selected, as in step 3, the selected pixels within the layer will be moved: if another selection tool (the Marquee or Lasso, for instance) is active, the selection area will move but not the pixels themselves. You can always hold `⌘` `ctrl` to access the Move tool temporarily while a selection or painting tool is active.

SHORTCUTS
MAC WIN BOTH

Concealing the evidence

1 The original board game was redrawn in Illustrator,
substituting appropriate room names for the original
drawing room, library, and so on. Redrawing the board also
allowed me to condense it so that the whole board fitted
into a smaller space.

WHILE ALL THE ELEMENTS OF A
photomontage need to be visible,
simply arranging the objects within the scene is
only the first step. To make the image both
realistic and appealing, it's important to add the
element of shadow.

This illustration for The Guardian was to
accompany a story about the candidates for the
top job at the British Broadcasting Corporation.
The political in-fighting led to the requirement
for a reproduction of a well-known murder
solving board game, in which the protagonists
were represented as suspects in the crime. In
the original game, the props were murder
implements – a candlestick, a gun, and so on. To
make the image more appealing, I replaced
these with TV-related paraphernalia. But
without the shadows, this illustration would
have appeared very flat indeed.

4 The shadows cast by the cards and objects were painted
onto a new layer with a soft brush. By using a pressure-
sensitive graphics tablet, I was able to achieve the effect of
smooth shading: I set the opacity of the brush quite low, and
then built up each shadow in the place where it would be
cast in real life.

2 The board was distorted using the Free Transform controls. An edge was drawn in to prevent the board looking too two-dimensional; the wooden table and black top were added on new layers.

3 The first suspect card was created in multiple layers, which were grouped into a layer set: this set was then duplicated to create each new card, and the resulting cards were arranged in the foreground in perspective. The TV elements are from a royalty-free collection, made shiny using the techniques described in Chapter 7. Compositionally, the image was now complete; but the whole looks very flat and unconvincing.

5 The far end of the board is visually less important, since all the main elements are clustered towards the front. Using the Gradient tool, again on a new layer, it was easy to draw a simple shadow fading from black to transparent. This shadow was also useful for the newspaper's art editor, as it gave him a clear space in which to place the headline.

6 The final step was to add 'mood lighting', in the form of bars of shadow that gave the impression of the board being lit through a barred window. Radiating lines were drawn as a selection using the Lasso tool, then feathered (a 20 pixel feather, in this instance) and, on a new layer, filled with black. Reducing the opacity of the whole layer allowed the detail to remain visible.

Visible light sources

1 Begin by adding a shadow to the scene. This is simply painted on a new layer, using a large soft-edged brush. Setting the brush to a low opacity allows us to paint the shadow on in small stages, being careful to leave an unshaded area where the light will eventually be cast.

S O FAR THIS CHAPTER has dealt with shadows cast by far-off light sources. When the light itself is in the frame, we obviously need to show it. In this workthrough, we're straying into the realms of hyper realism: by deliberately over emphasizing the visible light, the montage becomes more appealing than if we simply tried to reproduce reality. In real life, a light source wouldn't cast a visible beam unless the room were full of smoke; but then real life is often far duller than fiction.

Shadows are still important, for two reasons: firstly, because they add life to the image; and secondly, because a dark background will make the light itself stand out better. Here, we'll take the simple montage shown above and add both lighting and shadow to make it into a far more entertaining image.

4 Now exit QuickMask and, on a new layer, pick a pale yellow color (about 20% Yellow should do the trick) and then use the Gradient tool, set to Foreground to Transparent. Drag it from within the shade perpendicular to the shade edge, away from the lamp.

2 Next, we need to define the light. This is best drawn with the Pen tool, following the contour of the edge of the lamp shade and radiating outwards from the light source. Turn the path into a selection using ⌘ Enter ctrl Enter, then go into QuickMask to adjust the selected area.

3 In QuickMask, trace around the edges of the light area with the Lasso tool, omitting the edge around the shade. Then use Gaussian Blur to soften the edge – here, an 8-pixel radius blur was applied. Because the edge by the lamp shade was not selected, that part remains crisp and unblurred.

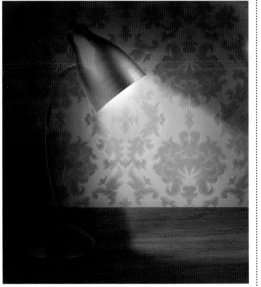

5 We now need an extra glow around the bulb itself. With the light area still selected, use a soft-edged brush to paint a spot of white at the focal point. Don't use a hard-edged brush: although bulbs are solid, you can't look at them when lit without seeing a haze around them.

6 Now we need to show the light acting upon the table surface. Using the Elliptical Marquee tool, draw an ellipse on the table. Feather the selection (an 8-pixel radius was used here), and delete that area from the shadow to return the table to its previous brightness.

HOT TIP

By using QuickMask to blur the light area, we're able to apply the blur just where we want it. If we'd simply feathered the selection instead, the whole area would have been blurred, leaving the light looking disconnected from the shade: this way, we're able to maintain the hard edge around the shade itself.

The romance of candlelight

CANDLES ARE UNIQUE light sources in that the light they cast is fully visible: you can stare straight at a candle without hurting your eyes. Because they shed so little light around them your eyes remain accustomed to the darkened environment, so when you do gaze at a candle's flame, you see a hazy glow around it.

Unlike metal lamp shades, candles are translucent objects. The light travels down through the candle and exits through the side, as well as radiating from the flame.

It would have been possible to begin this workthrough with a photograph of a candle. But I thought it would be more fun (and possibly more instructive) to draw our candle from scratch.

1 I drew this candle by drawing an elliptical marquee for the base, then duplicating it to create the top. I flattened the top ellipse to create a sense of perspective: the greater the difference between the two, the nearer the viewer is to the scene.

2 To join the two ellipses together, a rectangular selection was made between the half-way lines on each ellipse, and simply filled with the same color.

6 Before we create the flame, we need a background in order to see it. The shadows were added to this table and wall with a soft brush, leaving a fairly blank area where the flame would eventually appear.

7 For the shading on the candle itself, a new layer was created on top with its mode set to Multiply. This is because I used dark brown rather than black to shade it, which matches the candle color better.

3 The shading on the candle was added using the Burn tool set to Midtones: if it had been set to Highlights, it would have created a grayish shadow. The Dodge tool provided the highlight.

4 The dripping wax was drawn as a path with the Pen tool and then filled with yellow, although it would be possible to draw it directly with a hard-edged brush if you really can't get on with Bézier curves.

5 The shading on the drips was added using the Plastic Wrap filter – see Chapter 6, Shiny Surfaces, for more about this technique. The wick was simply drawn with the Brush, set to Dissolve to make a ragged outline.

8 The flame outline was drawn with the Pen tool, then the selection was feathered (a 4-pixel radius here) and filled with a mid orange hue.

9 With the Lock Transparency box checked, the white parts of the flame were painted on with a soft brush. In addition, a tiny blue patch was painted at the base of the flame for added realism.

10 Finally, a new layer was created behind the flame, and a glow added by painting a spot of yellow using a large, soft-edged brush set to a low opacity.

HOT TIP

The Plastic Wrap technique used for creating the drips of wax produced a grayish result that looked out of place. By locking the layer's transparency and using a brush set to Color mode, I was able to sample a color from the candle and paint that over the gray to return it to its true waxen hue.

Shading using Dodge & Burn

1 This girl has been photographed with even, direct lighting that's perfect for the photomontage artist: it's far better to start with flat lighting and add shading where you want it, than to have to make the whole illustration conform to one original.

PAINTING ON A SEPARATE LAYER is a good technique when adding shadows to walls, floors and many other kinds of inanimate objects, but the technique works badly when you're working with skintones: black shadows, even applied at a low opacity, can easily just turn to gray.

When working on the image of Mick Jagger above for the Sunday Times Magazine, I knew the direction the lighting was coming from – and it wouldn't change. If the positions of elements in a montage are known, then there's nothing to be lost by using the Dodge and Burn tools to add light and shade directly onto the image. But Dodge and Burn have three operating modes – Highlights, Midtones and Shadows; they each affect the image in different ways.

To be safe, work on a copy of the original layer: that way, if things go wrong, you can always get back to where you started.

5 The Dodge tool, set to Midtones, brightens up the other side of the face without destroying the original coloring. This is far more convincing for subtle tones, such as skin, than setting the tool's mode to Highlights.

2 Using the Burn tool to darken the side of the face, set to Highlights, results in a grayish tinge that's unappealing and unconvincing: it darkens the image, but also has a muting effect on the original skintones.

3 The Dodge tool, also set to highlights, has a rather different effect: it brightens up the image, but leaves a drastic impression on the colors. Those soft pinks and browns have turned to a vivid jaundiced yellow.

4 When set to Midtones, the Burn tool no longer loses color as it darkens the skin. Rather, the opposite is true: the shaded area quickly becomes strongly over-saturated as the shading is piled on.

6 Set to Shadows, both tools have an unfortunate effect on skin. The Dodge tool makes the shadows look like they've been doused in talcum powder, while the Burn tool turns the subject into a vision of the red death. Neither effect is what we want here.

7 The best technique is to use a combination of the two. Using a low opacity, use the tools set to Midtones first to retain the color; then switch to Highlights to paint the deep shadows in place. So far, so good; but the finished impression is rather over-enthusiastic, and needs toning down.

8 Lower the opacity of the painted-on layer, to allow the original to show through to some degree (you did work on a copy of the original layer, didn't you?). You can also use a layer mask to selectively hide portions of the shaded layer that now appear too strong.

HOT TIP

To avoid having to reach for the toolbox to switch between Dodge and Burn, there's a useful keyboard shortcut. When either of the tools is selected, holding down *ctrl* will temporarily select the other tool. I've mentioned this tip elsewhere in this book, and will continue to do so every time the Dodge and Burn tools crop up: it's an essential shortcut.

SHORTCUTS
MAC WIN BOTH

81

Shading using Light modes

SHADING USING THE THREE LIGHT MODES – Hard Light, Soft Light and Overlay – can have a far more cinematic effect than shading using the Dodge and Burn tools. But if Dodge and Burn are Nosferatu, then Hard Light is more Saturday Night Fever: shadows can take on a strong hue of their own. There are, of course, more than three light modes, especially in Photoshop 7; here are the main ones.

Rather than painting directly onto the layer, create a new layer and set it to Hard Light mode. You then have the option of filling the layer with 50% gray: this makes a good background when applying the shading to multiple layers. By filling your selection area with 50% gray and then locking the transparency, you can be sure that the light you paint will only be applied within the area where you want it.

If you must paint directly onto the layer, you can set the brush mode to Hard Light (or any of the other Light modes) to get the same results.

1 Be careful to use reasonably muted colors when painting shadows, or the effect will be too bright and unrealistic. This light blue is too bright for use either as shading or as a light reflection: it merely swamps the image with its color.

4 Now for the spotlight effect. Too bright a shade would have the unfortunate results shown in step 1 above; a muted brown gives us a color that lets the original skin texture show through, while adding a good amount of extra color to it.

2 Using a darker blue allows us to paint a shadow that's far more moody and evocative. This is the kind of shading that's often seen in films, where day-for-night shooting produces shadows that have a strong blue cast to them.

3 Switching to a strong pink gives us a good color with which to paint a transition on the face, between the shaded and the brightly lit areas. It's the effect produced by theatrical lighting, where colored gels are used instead of plain white lights to add emphasis to the actors' faces.

5 Here's the same effect set to Overlay mode instead. This is rather softer: the colors still have their effect on the image, but obscure the shading and texture of the original to a lesser degree.

6 More muted still is Soft Light mode, which produces an altogether subtler result. The three modes are variants of each other, and can be used in combination on different layers to build up the overall lighting effect.

HOT TIP

If you're using multiple colors when painting with Hard Light, as we are here, it's easy to apply the wrong color by accident – there's some trial and error involved in choosing shades that work. To prevent the possibility of losing a good effect, you can work on multiple Hard Light layers so that the effect is produced by the combination of all of them.

Lighting up: perfect neon

1 To begin with, create a new white layer beneath the basic lettering, and then merge the two. Then apply a Gaussian Blur until the hard corners are smoothed away. The actual amount will vary with the size and font chosen; I've used a blur radius of 4 pixels.

3 Select the pixels in the text layer using the Magic Wand tool and then, on a new layer, create a stroke outline using the Edit/Stroke menu. Don't use Layer Effects to make the stroke, or you won't be able to edit the outlines afterwards.

NEON LETTERING is one of those effects you can knock up in a few moments: simply create the outlines and add a glow to them. But to do it properly takes rather more time and patience.

The simplest way to create the smooth outlines for the lettering is to use the Round Corners feature in a program such as Illustrator. But since we're trying to work entirely in Photoshop, the technique described here – that of blurring and applying Levels – works just as well, and has the advantage that no additional software is required.

6 Now's a good time to add a background, with shadows as appropriate. I've also changed the color of the bottom row of text for the sake of interest, using Hue/Saturation. The next step is to make the outline look like tubing: this is achieved by darkening it with the Burn tool (set to Midtones) at the points where it's been strongly bent.

2 Now we can apply the Levels control to tighten up that blur. Open Levels and drag the small white and the small black triangles towards the center, and all the blurred area will turn to either pure white or pure black (see the screen grab, shown above right). If the whole group, including the

gray triangle, is dragged to the left the outlines will thicken up; dragged to the right, they'll thin out. Note that this effect only works when the text has been merged into a white layer: if the text had simply been blurred on its own, the Levels control would have had no effect.

The technique used here to soften the edges of lettering is one that was devised by Photoshop guru Kai Krause, before he went on to create the Kai's Power Tools range of plug-ins. He invented it as a way of cleaning up ragged artwork, such as faxed logos; but it's also perfect for rounding off text, and can even be used to apply rounded corners to a hard-edged outline.

4 Now hide the original text layer, and erase portions of the stroke to simulate the way neon lettering is constructed in the real world. Since all the lettering is made from a single bent glass tube, it needs to break within each letter where it turns to join the next letter.

5 To create the inner glow, select the layer's pixels by holding ⌘ *ctrl* and clicking on the name in the Layers palette. Use Edit/Select/Contract to reduce the selection size by, say, 3 pixels; then apply a 3-pixel Gaussian Blur to it. Now turn on the Lock Transparency checkbox, and fill the selected area with white.

7 The glow is created on a new layer, behind the tubing layer. First load up the pixels as outlined in step 5, then hold *Shift* ⌥ *Shift* *alt* as you enclose it with the Marquee tool to limit the selection to just the top word. Feather the selection (8 pixels used here), and fill with the same color as the tubing; then repeat with the bottom line of text.

8 The last step is to add the details. The wires are drawn on a new layer, shaded and shadowed using the technique shown in Chapter 9. One clip, which holds the lettering to the wall, was created on a separate layer; this clip was then copied around each letter in turn, rotated as appropriate so it appeared to grip the neon tubing.

Images on screens

1 This Palm Pilot is our starting point for the montage. The problem is that it was photographed with a screen full of icons: if we're to show just the text we want to display, we'll need to redraw the screen.

2 The first step is to outline the screen using the Pen tool or, if you have a steady hand, the Lasso tool (hold **⌐** *alt* as you go to make straight lines between click points). Make a new layer, and fill with a color sampled from the screen – in this case, I've used a color from the bottom right.

PLACING IMAGES ON TV or computer screens is no difficult matter: in the example above, the screen was curved slightly using the Shear filter and then distorted to fit the shape of the monitor.

When there's already an image on the screen, as in the Palm example on these pages, the problem becomes altogether trickier. Because we want to retain the screen furniture – the title bar and the scroll bar down the right hand side – we need to match the shading of the existing screen as much as possible. Here's how it's done.

6 To make the new screen blend with the old one, add a little Gaussian Noise: here, just 1% noise makes the difference between a screen that looks artificial and one that blends with the PDA. I've also used the Dodge tool, set to Midtones at a low opacity, to blend the top in more effectively. (If this tool is set to Highlights, you'll end up changing the colors of the screen as well as the shading.)

MEMO

Remember to take Palm on holiday

7 Now for our text. Type the text very small, with anti-aliasing turned off so that the result is the kind of jagged edges we associate with low resolution screens. The text here has been enlarged to show the effect. The smaller the text sized used, the stronger the jagged effect will be.

3 Now switch to the Gradient tool, set to Foreground to Transparent. Sample a color from the top right of the screen and drag that towards the center (making sure Preserve Transparency is checked).

4 Getting there - but the shading on the screen still doesn't quite match that of the original. Sample a shade from the left of the screen (you may need to hide the new layer first), and use the Gradient tool once again to drag this color in from the left.

5 Now for some fine-tuning. Using a large, soft brush set to a low opacity, sample some colors from the perimeter where the match is incorrect and dab the new colors in place.

8 Now rasterize the text (choose Rasterize Type from the Layer menu) so that it can be distorted freely. Use Free Transform (⌘ Shift T ctrl Shift T) to enlarge the text, and distort it by holding ⌘ ctrl as you drag each corner to make it match the perspective of the original screen.

9 Nearly there. The black text looked artificially strong; the trick is to sample a 'black' area of the original screen (such as the menu block top left) and fill the text with this color. Remember to check the Preserve Transparency box on the Layers palette first, or you'll end up flooding the whole window with the new color.

10 As a final step, we can reproduce the effect of the thickness of the glass. Duplicate the text layer, send it behind the original and lower its opacity to 20% for a faint shadow.

HOT TIP

A good trick for making images on TV screens more convincing is to add a pattern of fine horizontal white lines over the top, distorted to match the perspective of the monitor and reduced to a very low opacity. This reproduces the effect of old black-and-white televisions: even though color TVs don't use the line system in the same way, it's a visual code that signals to the reader that the image is on a screen.

SHORTCUTS
MAC WIN BOTH

Sourcing images

DIGITAL CAMERAS have provided Photoshop artists with the single most useful tool since Photoshop itself. They're now of a quality that makes them an essential accessory, and are available at a price that puts them within reach of almost everyone. The ability to capture an object and get it into Photoshop in seconds is unparalleled.

But there are some objects that aren't readily available to be photographed. Such items as space shuttles, polar bears and plates of roast turkey are notoriously hard to lay your hands on in a hurry. Fortunately, there's a solution: there's a huge amount of readily available imagery out there in the form of royalty-free photographic collections.

The images tend to be available in two ways: either as single images downloaded directly from websites, which will cost around $120 an image (but will be available immediately), or on collections of between 100 and 200 images on CD-ROM, costing an average of $400. The latter route obviously offers better value for money, but you have to plan your purchase well in advance of your 5pm deadline.

The quality of royalty-free images is almost uniformly high, but the type of material on offer is generally more suited to the designer than to the photomontage artist. You'll find dozens of CDs of stressed businessmen in high-tech offices, glamorous couples on tropical beaches and maps of the world cast in gleaming chrome – but these are all finished artwork, offering little scope for customizing. There are far fewer collections of cutout people and objects that can be used to form the basis of an original photomontage.

Among the best are sets of images from Stockbyte and PhotoDisc. The PhotoDisc images tend to feature glossy models who look like they've just walked out of a hairspray commercial, with the exception of one or two discs – their In Character CD, for example, is a collection of 100 people in a variety of costumes from medieval wizards to lion tamers. It's a CD I've used dozens of times, and it's saved me from having to clutter up my wardrobe with leopardskin thongs, deerstalkers and clown costumes. While it's easy enough to wear a suit and stand in front of a camera, exotic costumes are harder to find.

Stockbyte, on the other hand, produce a range of a dozen CDs in their Busy People series that feature everyday men, women, teenagers and children in a huge variety of poses. The people here are often old, ugly and badly dressed – in other words, just the sort of people you see on the streets. I've used images from the Busy People collection throughout this book. Two other CD-ROMs worth mentioning are Faces 2 from Rubber Ball, which contains 100 images of everyday people, and Bodyshots from Digital Wisdom, which includes over 300 images of businessmen and women in a variety of poses. The Bodyshots collection is one of the few to include a large number of people photographed from the side - although the lack of clipping paths (it's a very old collection) makes it harder to use.

Finding images of rare or even everyday objects used to be one of the hardest tasks of all. Stockbyte and PhotoDisc both produce CDs of office equipment, household items and more; but the range of possible objects is vast, and 100 images per disk can barely hope to supply everything we need. Now, however, Canadian publisher Hemera has produced two sets of images in the Hemera Photo-Objects 50,000 collections. The lightning-fast visual search engine produces results even before you've finished typing the name of the object you're looking for, and it's a fair bet that almost any object you need will be found among the hundred thousand on offer. (When I first got the collection I asked everyone walking past to think of an object to look for: I thought I'd found their weak spot when someone suggested 'Hubble space telescope'. I searched, and there were seven images.) Even more astonishingly, each 50,000 strong volume is available for under $100. There is, of course, a downside: the images are of uniformly low resolution, supplied up to a maximum of 1200 x 1200 pixels. But when used as small elements in a larger montage, there's no better starter kit.

5 Heads and bodies

PHOTOMONTAGE ARTISTS are frequently asked to put one person's head on another person's body. When creating montages using politicians or celebrities, it's unusual to find the original head attached to a body that suits the requirements of the finished image. In this chapter, we'll look at how to make heads and bodies join seamlessly together. Eye contact, as we discussed in Chapter 3, is crucial to making characters relate to one another. So here's a technique for changing the direction your subject is looking in.

Hair has always been a problem in montage creation. We can't always work with Telly Savalas or Yul Brynner; those flyaway strands always seem to get in the way. In this chapter we'll look at how to ease the pain of cutting hair from its background.

Making the head fit

1 Begin by cutting out the head, using the Pen tool to create a clean Bézier path. To make the montage work, it's important to make it the same size and orientation as the head on the target body: it helps to place the two side by side, so the new head can be adjusted to fit.

PUBLICITY PHOTOGRAPHS of celebrities and politicians tend to be either highly staged or snatched papparazzi images. This portrait of George W Bush, which we'll use several times in this chapter, is a prime example of the former: immaculately groomed and lit, it's the kind of image you'd see adorning a thousand Republican walls.

From the point of view of the photomontage artist, it's the perfect shot. The three-quarter view means that it can be used on bodies both head-on and in near profile: we can make this president do almost anything we choose using a few simple Photoshop tricks. First, we'll look at the best way to give him a new body.

You'll notice that Bush's hair on the cutout doesn't have the hard edge associated with Pen tool cutouts. We'll look in detail about how to cut out hair later in this chapter.

4 Now we need to hide those parts of the original head that showed through behind that of Bush. Using a layer mask is the best way to achieve this, as we can always paint back areas we want to keep later. If you feel confident, you can always simply delete the head instead.

IMAGES: US DEPARTMENT OF DEFENSE ; BODYSHOTS

Hue/Saturation

Edit: Master

Hue: 7

Saturation: -20

Lightness: -5

OK
Cancel
Load...
Save...

☐ Colorize
☑ Preview

2 The next step is to match the skintones of the body we're pasting this head onto. There are several ways of changing colors - you can use Curves, Color Balance, Levels, and so on. Here, we'll use the Hue/Saturation dialog to make the adjustments we need.

3 Because all fair skins fall within a similar tonal range, only small color adjustments need to be made: raising the Hue setting by just 7 loses that red tinge. More important is the need to reduce the Saturation of the over lit original; the Lightness has also been reduced slightly.

5 Next, we need to make a layer mask for Bush. Using a small, soft-edged brush, paint out a smooth line beneath the chin so that the head and neck blend seamlessly together. For more on layer masks, see Chapter 2, Hiding and Showing.

6 Bush has been lit from the right, where the body was lit from the left – which is why we were left with that unconvincing bright spot on the neck. Make a new layer, and group it with the body layer; then sample a dark shade from the side of Bush's face, and paint in a shadow on the neck.

HOT TIP

When matching bodies to heads, try to choose combinations that have been photographed from as similar an angle as possible. While you can place just about any head on just about any body, the more extreme differences of view will make the montage less plausible.

Matching skintones

1 The somewhat startled look on this bodybuilder's head may imply some prescience that he's about to be decapitated. But we can't let ethical considerations get in the way of a good montage: out with the muscleman, in with the politician.

3 Bush's neck is blended into the body using a layer mask once again. Take care to remove enough of the neck so that no join is visible: remember that when using a brush in the layer mask, you can use the **X** key to switch foreground and background colors, and so paint back areas you've painted out.

WHEN THERE'S NO SUIT to hide behind, matching skintones means making the lighting match as well. With no collar to tuck the neck into, it's more important than ever to make sure the colors and tones blend together seamlessly. Here, we'll give George W a shiny new body.

5 Because the original image was lit directly from the front, with no side shading visible, it's easier to remove the shadow on Bush's head than to try to add shadows to the complex musculature of the body. But using the Dodge tool set to Highlights produces this garish, oversaturated effect.

IMAGES: US DEPARTMENT OF DEFENSE, DIGITAL VISION

2 Once again, we begin by matching the size of the new head to that of the old. This time, however, we want to make Bush's head slightly larger than the original, so he doesn't end up looking too much like a pinhead.

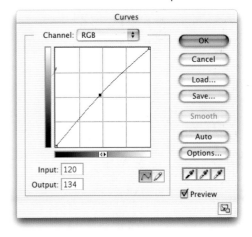

4 The color of Bush's face matches that of the body pretty well: all we really need to do is to brighten it up slightly. Open the Curves dialog, click a point midway along the diagonal line, and drag it vertically upward by a small amount to make the change.

6 Instead, change the mode of the Dodge tool to Midtones by holding *ctrl* *Shift* *Shift* right click and selecting Midtones from the pop-up menu. Stick to a low opacity and paint slowly – you can set the opacity by pressing the number keys, using 1 for 10%, 4 for 40% and so on, up to 0 for 100%.

HOT TIP

If you delete the head from the body before adding the new head, be sure to leave enough neck to graft the new head onto: to be safe, only delete from the mouth line upwards.

SHORTCUTS

95

Matching picture graininess

1 The original photograph of Bill Clinton clearly shows the grain in the image. We need to match that to make the montage work successfully.

2 Once again, Bush's head is scaled to the right size to fit this body. His expression is perfect for the new pose.

WHEN ONE PRESIDENT replaces another, why go to all the trouble of getting the photographers in for a special photo session? Photoshop, after all, can do the job just as well in far less time.

This body may suit George W Bush better than that in the previous example, but there are other concerns here. The original picture was very grainy, and when we zoom in we can see that grain more clearly. I admit, I've enhanced the grain using Unsharp Mask to show the problem better - but you don't always expect the truth when politicians are involved.

6 We're lucky here in that there's a large, flat area of the image that we can use to sample the grain: it's the expanse of gray around the seal on the front of the podium. Make a rectangular selection into a new layer.

7 The piece of grain was still too small – but we can't stretch it, or the grain will be the wrong size. Tile it by duplicating the selection and flipping it horizontally, then duplicating the result and flipping it vertically.

3 Bush's head is corrected for color using the Curves dialog, and a layer mask is used to blend the two images. We still need to get rid of the remnants of the previous president.

4 Hide Bush and make a new layer to paint the patch into. Set the Clone tool to sample All Layers, and clone out the parts of Clinton that were visible behind Bush's head.

5 With Bush firmly in place, the glaring discrepancies between the grainy original and the sharp portrait are even more obvious. Time to fix that grain.

8 After grouping the new grain with Bush's head, knock all the color out using the Desaturate command ⌘ U ctrl U. Then brighten it up using Curves so that the overall shade is roughly 50% black.

9 When the mode of this layer is set to Hard Light (chosen from the pop-up menu at the top of the Layers palette), we can see through it to the head beneath: the midtones vanish, leaving just shadows and highlights.

10 Because the effect was a little strong, it needs to be toned down by reducing the opacity of the layer. The amount you choose depends on the individual image: here, I've reduced it to 50% opacity.

HOT TIP

You won't always be lucky enough to find a flat section of the image from which to copy the grain. In cases where there's no suitable region available, make a new layer and fill it with 50% gray, then apply the Noise filter; the layer can then be scaled until the grain matches that of the original image.

SHORTCUTS

The perfect haircut

CUTTING OUT HAIR has always been a tricky task for the Photoshop user. Several third-party plug-ins, such as Extensis Mask Pro and Corel Knockout, have attempted to make the job easier; Knockout comes closer than most, although it still isn't an easy tool to use.

The introduction of the Background Eraser tool in Photoshop made the complex removal of backgrounds easier than it had ever been before. It's a tool that works best with hair and other loose objects photographed against a plain, preferably white background; even then, it can be a fiddly activity, and its success depends in large part upon the kind of background the image will eventually have. Users who find the prospect daunting should skip to the next section, where I'll explain how to cheat with hair.

1 This stock image has been photographed against a plain, near-white background. It's the ideal candidate for cutting the hair using the Background Eraser tool.

2 First cut out the image loosely, leaving a margin around the hair. I find it useful to make a new layer filled with a solid color, so you can see more clearly what's being erased.

4 Start working your way around the head. The crosshairs in the center of the tool pick up the color that will be erased; everything within the circle radius is removed.

5 Sometimes, the tool will erase areas you wanted to keep – such as the highlights within the shoulder at the right of this figure. That's where Protect Foreground Color comes in.

9 With all the background erased, you'll probably be left with a figure whose hair has a definite bright tinge to it. It was, after all, photographed against white.

10 If you're going to end up with your figure on a light or complex background, this may be sufficient: you won't notice that the edges are brighter than the middle.

Brush size: Don't
use too large a
brush, or you'll
erase white areas
such as the eyes
and teeth.

Limits: Set to
Discontiguous to
erase background
areas surrounded
by hair.

Tolerance: Set
too low, the brush
won't erase the
background; too
high and you'll
lose too much
hair.

Protect
Foreground
Color: Use this to
sample skin tones
as you work
around the head.

Sampling: Stick
to Once when
working with a
plain background,
Continuous if the
background is
varied.

3 Access the Background Eraser tool
by choosing it from the pop-up
menu that appears when you hold the
mouse button down on the Eraser tool
in the toolbar. There are several

parameters that need to be considered.
We'll use the Discontiguous setting,
which allows the tool to erase
background areas that are totally
enclosed by other colors; and we'll set

the sampling to Once, since the
background is a single flat color. The
Tolerance depends on the contrast
between the hair and the background:
experiment to get the best setting.

6 Hold down ⌥ alt and click on
the shoulder color: it will become
the foreground color, and will not be
erased. You'll need to keep resampling
as you work round the head.

7 Sometimes, even protecting a
foreground color can't stop some
bright areas from being erased – such
as the highlights around the eyebrow
seen here.

8 The solution is to use the History
palette. Choose the History brush,
and click next to the step immediately
before: you can now paint the erased
areas back in again.

HOT TIP

Using the Clone
tool to copy hair
texture from
one area to
another is a
fiddly job,
because you
need to make
sure the strands
of hair you're
copying from lie
in the same
orientation as
those you're
copying to. For
some tasks, it
may be simpler
to copy locks of
hair to a new
layer, group
them with the
base layer and
twist them to
make the hair
fall the right
way.

11 If your background is dark,
however, the bright hair fringe
will look awkward and out of place.
There are two ways of solving this,
depending on your patience.

12 The easiest way is simply to
use the Burn tool set to
Highlights, and darken the edges of the
hair. With luck, no-one will notice that
it doesn't really look like hair.

13 To do the job properly, use the
Clone tool. Check the Lock
Transparency box and work your way
around, cloning hair texture from
within the hair to cover the edges.

SHORTCUTS

The solution for flyaway hair

1 Start by creating a smooth cutout of the hair, being careful not to include any of the background. If you use images from royalty-free libraries or CD collections, you'll find that in most cases the clipping path will cut just inside the hair edge, making them perfect for this technique.

T HIS COVER FOR THE SUNDAY TIMES
magazine was a surprisingly complex
montage – the owl and background were two
separate layers, and no less than four images
were comped together to make Harry Potter. His
original hair was cut out using the techniques
shown on the previous pages; but to make it
more windswept, I added stray strands using the
Smudge tool, as shown here.

The Smudge tool is by far the quickest way of
creating a soft hair effect. On the following
pages, we'll look at an even faster way of
applying this tool: here, though, are the basics
of hair smudging.

4 So far, so good: but the hair strands all have the same length. For a more natural feel, increase the opacity of the brush and pull out one or two hairs at random to a greater length. It really helps to use a pressure-sensitive graphics tablet for this job!

2 Use the Smudge tool, set to a small brush size, with an opacity of around 70% (you can also use a Spatter brush - see the following page). Begin at the crown and work down one side of the head, smudging from the hair outwards, tweaking out individual strands as you go.

3 Now go back to the crown and work the other way, making sure you follow the direction of the hair as you brush. It helps to have a few hairs sticking straight out of the crown, where there's a transition between the hair growing in different directions.

5 If the strands of hair begin to look too drawn, then lock the transparency of the layer and use the Clone tool to copy some of the hair texture from within the head onto the edge area.

6 When viewed against a white background, hair treated in this way will always tend to look a little fabricated. But when placed against any texture or image, it will blend in perfectly: the translucence of the hair strands will pick up any background it's positioned on.

HOT TIP

Work slowly, starting from the top and progressing down both sides of the figure. If you work upwards, you'll find your Smudge strokes will distort hairs you've already drawn, resulting in unnatural kinks and whirls. If the hair you draw looks too wild, it's easy to smooth the edges by erasing them with a soft-edged eraser.

Short back and sides

1 Where the Background Eraser tool works well for images photographed against a plain background, the flag behind George W Bush is far too complex an image to be able to erase it easily.

THE INTERNET MADE EASY: this image for .net magazine would have been almost impossible to create if I'd tried to cut out the fur using the Background Eraser tool. Even the technique described on the previous pages would have taken an age: drawing out each strand on this furry body would have been far too time-consuming.

But a hard, cutout edge would have looked phoney and unrealistic; I needed a way to make the fur look real.

The technique described on these pages is by far the quickest and easiest way to make hair look more natural. It doesn't take long to use the Smudge tool in the way described here to work all the way around the edge of your chosen animal - and it works for people too.

4 As before, begin at the crown and work down one side of the head. A well-groomed head such as this doesn't need a lot of loose strands, so set the Smudge tool to a medium opacity – 50% to 70% will work. With this brush you'll draw out multiple strands, rather than one at a time.

2 Begin, as before, by cutting out the figure smoothly using the Pen tool. When preparing hair, always make a new layer from the base image first: otherwise, you'll find it impossible to get your chosen background to fit.

3 This time, we'll use one of the Spatter brushes that are built into the Photoshop brush set by default. Hold *ctrl* *Shift* *Shift* right click to choose the brush: the size of brush depends on the size of the image you're working on.

5 Now repeat the process for the other side of the head, again working from top to bottom. If you have the patience, you can once again lock the transparency of the layer and use the Clone tool to copy the hair texture to the strands you've just created.

6 If you prefer your politicians a little more windswept, simply use a larger Spatter brush or set the Smudge tool to a higher opacity. Wild hair makes people look more emotional and less in control: ideally, you'd need wild eyes with hair such as this – which we'll come to later.

HOT TIP

Always bear in mind the way hair grows when tweaking out strands using this technique. Even well cut hair won't always lie in exactly the direction the hairdresser intended; pull some strands against the flow for a more natural look.

SHORTCUTS
MAC WIN BOTH

103

The problem of hair loss

DAVID DUCHOVNY growing older, in stages: the image above, for Focus magazine, was always intended to be more cartoony than realistic.

We'll look at how to achieve an ageing effect in a more authentic and plausible manner on the following pages. For now, though, let's just see how easy it is to turn a full head of hair into a shining bald pate, using our customary model. When you're ready, Mr President – and I promise this will be the last time I use George W Bush in this chapter. ·

1 Begin by making an elliptical selection from whatever forehead is visible. Make the selection as large as you can without going into the hair line, then turn it into a new layer using ⌘ J ctrl J and place it roughly in position.

5 Next, we can turn that smoothed-out hair into more realistic strands using the Smudge tool, as described on the previous pages. The difference here is that rather than smudging the hair itself, we're smudging the mask: we're not creating new strands, but revealing those we'd painted out.

2 Stretch the ellipse to form the shape of the dome of the head. Because we copied the original forehead, we can be sure that the skin tones, textures and lighting will match perfectly.

3 Now make a layer mask and, using a soft-edged brush, paint out along the bottom of the layer so that it blends smoothly into the original forehead. For more on layer masks, see Chapter 2, Hiding and Showing.

4 Now for the hair. Make a layer mask once again, and paint out the hair behind the bald dome so that it recedes in a natural manner. Using a layer mask, it's easy to paint back areas that were erased accidentally.

6 The bald dome needs a little work with the Clone tool to remove the obviously stretched forehead lines. Now is also a good time to add a slight shine to the top of the head, using the Dodge tool set to Midtones to avoid changing the colors.

7 We can now put the newly bald Bush back on his original background. The trouble is, the hair on the original still shows through; but it's easy enough to get rid of, as we'll see in the next step.

8 Even with a complex background such as this, we can use the Clone tool to replicate stars and paneling from one area and place them behind the head. Back on his original background, George W looks more at home than ever.

The ageing process

ADDING A FEW YEARS onto a celebrity's image is a process that involves several steps. Graying up the hair is an obvious starting point; but there are other, more subtle indications of advancing years.

In this workthrough we're going to take a photograph of Prince Charles taken in the days when he was a carefree bachelor, and bring it up to date – and maybe project his image a few years into the future.

Making a person bald as they age is one possibility, but the results can be too extreme – and can often make the image look too jokey. In this case, we're going to age Prince Charles while keeping his full thatch of hair intact.

1 The original image of Charles was taken some years ago, as can be sen from his youthful good looks and chestnut-brown hair.

2 We'll begin by selecting the hair. Go into QuickMask mode by pressing **Q** and select the hair by painting around it with a soft-edged brush. We don't need to worry about being too accurate at this stage. Exit QuickMask, and make a new layer from the selection using **⌘ J** **ctrl J**.

6 As people age, their features coarsen. Ears, in particular, tend to enlarge with time. Select the ear, using QuickMask again, make a new layer from it and then stretch it slightly using Free Transform.

7 Bags under the eyes are a sure sign of age. Rather than drawing a new bag from scratch, it makes more sense to use what's already there. Select the eye bag (QuickMask again) and make a new layer from it; then stretch it with Free Transform so that it reaches further down the cheek. You need to be careful when doing this to make sure none of the original bag is visible, or it will look unconvincing.

3 The hair is brightened up using the Curves dialog (although you could just as well used Levels or even Brightness and Contrast instead). The color is then knocked out of it using the Hue/Saturation dialog: drag the Saturation slider to the left to reduce the amount of color in the hair.

4 In the last step, some of the forehead and ear was brightened up along with the hair. We can now remove this by making a new layer mask, and painting out the unwanted bright areas.

5 Decades of shaving tends to leave its mark on the face. We can accentuate this by selecting the beard area in QuickMask, making a new layer from it, and then adding Gaussian Noise and reducing the saturation so that it appears grayish.

When creating multiple layers that all act upon base artwork, it makes sense to group each new layer with the base as you create it. That way you'll avoid the problem of fine elements – such as the veins in step 9 or the shading in step 10 – from leaking out around the edge of the head.

8 To accentuate the wrinkles, duplicate the base layer (so you can return to it if you need to) and use the Burn tool to trace in the lines around the eyes and nose. Add subtle lines on the forehead using a low opacity, and add some wrinkles into the neck for good measure. By using the Burn tool set to Midtones, we can avoid the color loss that we'd have got if it had been set to Highlights.

9 The next stage is a subtle one: drawing in the fine veins that appear on the cheek and nose as we get older. On a new layer, use a very small Brush and paint using a dark red. Short, wiggly strokes will create the effect we want with little effort.

10 The final step is to knock out some of the rosy color from his face. Make a new layer, and set its mode to Color: then, using a soft brush set to a very low opacity – around 20% works well – paint with white to reduce the ruddy complexion. Be careful not to overdo it at this stage: we want our celebrity to look older, but not necessarily decrepit. Even British royalty can grow old gracefully.

SHORTCUTS

It's all in the eyes

THIS ILLUSTRATION FOR LISTINGS magazine Time Out shows two newsreaders slugging it out in competition for the ten o'clock news program. Both men had been photographed head-on, and the head of Sir Trevor McDonald (in the red shorts) barely fits the profile body. But by moving the eyes of both so that they stared at each other, it was possible to create some emotional interaction between them that would have been lacking if they'd remained gazing at the viewer.

In the chapter Composing the Scene we looked at how important eye contact is – which means having the ability to move eyes at will. Here, we'll take one of the figures used in that chapter and show how to prepare the eyes so that people can be made to look in any direction you choose.

1 This figure has eyes that are wide enough for us to be able to position the eyeballs wherever we choose. More importantly, there's enough of the pupil visible to allow us to use it later. Begin by making a circular selection that encompasses the pupil.

4 Turn the path into a selection by pressing ⌘ Enter ctrl Enter, then make a new layer named Eyeball and fill the selected area with white. This will form the basis for our new eyeball.

7 We can now show the pupil layer again. Position it above the Eyeball layer and group it using ⌘ G ctrl G, so that we only see the pupil where it overlaps the eyeball. Select the pupil and drag a copy (by holding ⌥ alt as you drag) until both are looking in the same direction.

2 Make a new layer from the selection using ⌘ J / *ctrl* J, then duplicate the layer and flip it vertically. Now erase the eyelid showing on the new layer, and continue erasing until the two halves of the pupil become one. When the eyeball looks convincing, merge the two layers.

3 Hide the new pupil – we'll come back to it later. Now, using the Pen tool, draw a Bézier path around each eyeball. Use as few points as possible for a smooth outline: I try to use anchor points just in the corners of each eye, making the path handles do all the work.

5 Add shading around the edge of the eyeball using the Burn tool set to Highlights, using a low opacity. Build up the shading slowly, so that it doesn't appear too harsh.

6 The original shading appeared to have a bluish tint, although in fact it was purely gray. Use Color Balance to add a little red and a little yellow to the eyeball, then soften the edges using the Blur tool.

8 So far, so good: but the eyes still don't look real. The solution is to change the layer mode of the pupils from Normal to Multiply, so that the shading we applied to the eyeballs shows through onto the pupils. It's a subtle difference, but it completes the effect.

9 With both eyes now complete, we can move the pupils independently of the eyeballs to make them look in any direction we choose. Because the two layers are grouped together, the pupils always appear to move within the range of the eyeballs.

HOT TIP

It isn't always possible to lift the original pupils from a face: sometimes the eyes are just too closed to be able to see them clearly. In cases like these, it's worth taking a pupil from another image (keeping it handy for future use), and simply dragging it into the composition. You can change the color of the eyes using the Hue/Saturation dialog, so that they match the original.

SHORTCUTS
MAC WIN BOTH

Sleep and the art of healing

1 The first step in using the Healing tool is to specify the clone target. Hold the ⌥ *alt* key and click on the point you want to clone from. Choose an area of skin that's relatively free from wrinkles, lines and stubble, such as the cheek in this example.

ONE OF THE MAIN NEW FEATURES in Photoshop 7 is the Healing tool. Designed for the removal of noise and scratches from photographs, it can also be used for more wide-reaching applications: a prime example might be to remove the hole left by the earring in the model on the right.

Here, we're going to use the tool to make this figure look like he's sleeping. If I'd had Photoshop 7 when doing the illustration above for Time Out (about the tedium of royal weddings) I'd have made a far more convincing job of it. Now, in just a few steps, we can close our model's eyes far more easily: with the new Voice Annotation feature in Photoshop 7, we can even add the sound of snoring.

4 Repeat the process for the other eye. There's no need to specify the target point again, since this will be chosen automatically. Once again, the eyelid appears too bright while we're in the process of using the healing tool – but this will be corrected when the button is released.

2 Now begin to paint over the area you want to heal. As you paint, the target area will be cloned directly, as shown here – and it will appear badly shaded as a result. Avoid healing over the bottom eyelashes, as they'll mark the closure of the eye.

3 Once you release the mouse button, the cloned area will take on the light and shade characteristics of the area you healed into. Note how the eyelid, previously far too bright, has now toned in well with the area of skin that lies around it.

5 With both eyelids now fully healed, we can see how the shading closely matches the surrounding skin. The problem now is that the eyelids have taken on the color values of the open eyes, resulting in a grayish hue that looks a little artificial.

6 This is easily fixed by using a soft-edged paint brush set to Color mode, and painting over the eyelids with a color sampled from nearby. Now, our previously wide-awake figure looks like he's sleeping peacefully.

HOT TIP

Because you don't see the full effect of the Healing tool until after you've finished painting (and after Photoshop has processed the result), you can't always see what you're doing as you go along. It's often best taken in short steps, alternating between large and small brushes as you go, so you can watch the result build up in stages.

SHORTCUTS
MAC WIN BOTH

The freelance artist

FOR THE FREELANCER, working at home is one of the main attractions of the job. It can also be one of the major drawbacks.

The advantages are plentiful. No need to worry about bus and train times; no commuting; and above all, no office politics. On the down side, there's the problem that you're always at work, even when you're off-duty. In order to complete this book I had to rent a flat at the seaside simply to get away from the telephone: it's hard to complete a long-term project when the telephone's constantly offering you short-term work.

When you work at home, it's important that you have a separate room in which to work. Partly it's because you need somewhere you know won't be littered with washing, children's toys and bicycle parts; but mainly, so there's somewhere you can go out of in the evening. In the days when I used to have my computer set up in the back of the living room I felt I could never get away from it.

I now never work at weekends. It's a golden rule that I break only two or three times a year, and even then it's only when I'm called out to deliver a talk or work on the help desk at a Mac show. I occasionally have to turn work down that would require me to work over a weekend to meet a deadline, but my sanity is all the better for the restriction.

Try to arrange your workspace so that your desk faces the window, so the light doesn't glare on the screen, and make sure you use sidelights rather than ceiling lights for the same reason. Don't push your desk right up against the wall or window: you'll need to get round the back to plug in cables, and you want to make this as easy as possible.

I'd also recommend renting a water cooler. Partly because water's good for you; but mainly because since I got mine my coffee intake has dropped considerably. And, at the risk of sounding like your mother, I'd also suggest eating lunch now and again. Falling over from hunger at 4.30 in the afternoon will do little to help you meet a 6pm deadline.

There are two main problems with the freelance lifestyle: not having enough work, and having too much. It's hard to decide which is the more onerous: if you don't have enough work, you can always spend the spare time putting up shelves. But if you have too much, at some point you'll get to that dreaded stage when you realize that you'll have to turn a job away.

The first time you turn work down it feels awful: after all, there's a job that needs doing, and if you don't do it they'll get someone else – so what will happen next time? Will they come back to you, or go straight to the person they know could get it done last time? The answer is that if you're any good, people will come back; and if you're too much in demand to do the work one week, they'll be all the more keen next time. But if you take on more than you can handle, you'll do neither job well.

There are many factors that determine whether a freelance artist gets plenty of work: whether your work's any good, whether it's original, whether you can interpret a brief, and so on. But without doubt the strongest factor is this: can you meet a deadline?

Unlike trains, TV shows and your brother's birthday, you can't miss a deadline. Period. If a newspaper phones you at 1pm and requires an illustration delivered by 5pm, then that's the time you have to have it finished. It's no good spending an extra couple of hours turning your illustration into a work of art if the paper's gone to press by the time you've finished: they'll be faced with a blank page, which they'll fill with a stock photograph, and the phone will go strangely silent for the next few weeks.

The tightest deadline I ever had was 45 minutes, for an illustration for the front page of a newspaper: it ended up with me right up against the deadline, asking for an extra ten minutes and being granted five. The next day a quarter of a million copies were distributed around the country, each one showing the bits I hadn't finished yet; the day after that it was lining the bottom of the cat litter tray. So much for posterity.

6 Shiny surfaces

GLASS, WE'RE TOLD, is really a liquid. Which is little consolation when you're traversing a glass-floored walkway, but the resemblance between the two can be a great help when you're working in Photoshop.

Glass and liquids share many properties in common: they both reflect and refract light, and they can both be drawn more easily than you might have thought possible. In this chapter we'll look at some of the different ways of creating glazed objects, from bottles and windows to the floor of a fashion catwalk.

Introducing... Miracle Wrap

THE PLASTIC WRAP FILTER is one of the most useful special effects Photoshop has to offer. Use it to make anything glisten – from beads of sweat on a dancer's forehead to visceral internal organs (see the Case Study on the following pages). Oh, and if you really want to, you can also use it to draw plastic wrapping.

In this workthrough, we're going to use Plastic Wrap to create shiny, dripping paint on the can shown above, although exactly the same technique could be used to draw coffee, blood or just about anything that dribbles.

1 The first step is to draw the drip. The best way of doing this is to use the Pen tool to draw an editable Bézier path: but if you're uncomfortable with that tool, use the Brush instead – although it's harder to create smooth curves with the Brush tool.

Fill with a midtone gray (or paint with gray if you're using the Brush). There's no point worrying about color at this stage; all we need to do us to create a base that's suitable for the Plastic Wrap filter.

2 Now comes the tricky part: preparing the artwork for the filter. The best way to begin is to shade the drips, using the Dodge and Burn tools, so that it looks vaguely three-dimensional. (Remember, if you hold ⌥ *alt* while using the Burn tool, it temporarily Dodges – a real time saver.)

Next, create some random light and dark patches in the larger areas of the paint splash. There's no exact science to this, since the Plastic Wrap filter works in mysterious and sometimes unfathomable ways; only experimentation will show you which techniques work and which don't.

3 Time for Plastic Wrapping. The settings don't make an enormous amount of difference to the end result, but play around with them – you can see the changes instantly.

Because the original shading can affect the filter's result so dramatically you can't expect to just draw, filter and have done with it. So try this: do some shading, perform the filter, and see how it looks. Then undo, shade some more (or step back through the Histories to shade less) and apply the filter again. And again. This one can take some time to get right.

4 Brightness and Contrast always help a filter like this – the more glistening and shiny, the better. The drips look OK, but that pool of paint at the bottom was a little unconvincing; to fix it, I drew an elliptical selection and added ripples using the ZigZag filter (which, for some reason, creates ripples, unlike the Ripple filter, which doesn't).

Because I used Lock Transparency to prevent the ZigZag filter from distorting the edges of my lovely curves, I needed to clone some of the original image back where the filter had filled bits with white. No problem – that's what the History brush is there for.

5 Finishing touches. The blue color was made with a solid blue layer, grouped with the drip and set to Hard Light, 70% opacity. This is a more effective method than simply using Hue and Saturation or even Curves to put the color in, since we want to add a solid wash rather than merely tinting the gray.

Shadows were added both beneath the drips and around the edges to make it look more three-dimensional. Finally, I took the lid off the paint can so we could see some of the paint inside by creating a lid-shaped selection on a new layer, shading it and then adding a drop of paint color.

HOT TIP

Performing a filter such as Plastic Wrap will change the look of the base layer completely. Always take a copy of the layer before applying the final filter effect to it, so you can revert and make changes if you need to later.

SHORTCUTS
MAC WIN BOTH

117

Blood and gore, no sweat

1 The original image, generated from a 3D model, may have been a useful teaching aid – but there was no way this would look like a convincing heart as it stood. As with most basic 3D modeling, this one looks like it's made of plastic rather than flesh and blood. This is the kind of application at which Plastic Wrap excels.

THE BRIEF for this illustration was to produce a realistic image of a heart, to be used on the front page of The Guardian. I was supplied with an image of a basic 3D model; it had everything in the right place, but looked like the model it was. I immediately asked if the illustration had to be accurate enough to fool heart surgeons: 'No,' came the reply, 'it only has to fool Guardian readers.' A much simpler proposition altogether.

2 The first step was to desaturate the image. Then, after locking transparency (so the edges didn't fuzz up), I appled Gaussian Blur to smooth out the veins.

3 The first application of Plastic Wrap picked up the contours and added a shiny, glistening tone to the image - without a brushstroke having been added.

4 The image was colorized using Hue/Saturation to give it a base color on which to build. Already, it was starting to look far more real and organic.

5 A second application of Plastic Wrap was added, which was then masked out selectively over areas where it seemed too strong - mainly the large expanses of flat aorta.

6 The veins were painted in on a new layer using Hard Light mode, which allowed the underlying texture to show through; the tubes and pipes at the top were painted on a layer set to Color mode.

7 Finally, the plumbing at the top was copied to a new layer (by using a soft brush in QuickMask to ensure smooth edges) and then brightened up and tinted to look convincing.

HOT TIP

When working on an image like this, it helps to create multiple layers for coloring and tinting the different areas: that way, the strength of each layer can easily be reduced by simply lowering the opacity of the layer. Group each new layer with the base layer to make sure no color leaks out around the edges.

119

Water, water everywhere

1 This straightforward suburban scene is about to be flooded by water. The differing angles across the image will involve treating both the water and the reflections to follow the perspectives of the original image, as we'll see over the next few steps.

ART EDITORS LOVE SUBMERGING THINGS. Whether it's a computer (Dotcom Firms Sink Without Trace), a confused businessman (Is Stress Swallowing You Up?) or an entire city (Global Warming: Life in 2050), they just can't get enough of floods.

The image above was fairly trivial to create: the island scene was simply reflected vertically, and the sun and sky reflection placed behind it. The strong ripples in the water helped to conceal any rough edges.

In this section we'll look at a slightly more complicated flood, which involves reflections as well as submerging.

4 Now the water needs to run along the walls that sit perpendicular to the one at the front. Because we made a layer mask in the first instance, rather than simply deleting the water, it's easy enough to paint it back in again, following the contours of the bricks as a guide.

7 Next, the sections of wall that face away from us are copied and again distorted into place. This includes elements such as the pink gate, which clearly lies in a different plane to the front of the wall.

2 First, find yourself some water. This image was taken
from a photograph of the sea, from which the sky has
simply been deleted: water can be devilishly tricky stuff to
draw, so it's worth finding a real picture if you can.

3 The first step in making the water fit the scene is to
decide on the level at which it will sit. Make a new layer
mask (Reveal All) for the water, and paint it out along an
obvious perspective line: here, the brick wall at the front
provides a useful horizontal to set the water on.

5 The original water was far too bright: it had been
photographed on a sunny day, when there was plenty of
blue sky for it to reflect. In this urban setting, the sky would
be minimal, so its saturation needs to be reduced using the
Hue/Saturation dialog.

6 The background is copied in sections, flipped vertically
and grouped with the water, using the techniques
described in Glass Reflections later in this chapter. First, the
sides facing us – the front of the wall and the wall holding
the door – are flipped and distorted into place.

8 But the surface of the water is rippled, not flat; so the
reflections need to be distorted as well. Here, the Wave
filter (appropriately enough) has been used to add a small
amount of rippling to the reflected image. I've also reduced
the opacity of the ripples for a better effect.

9 As well as reflecting the scene above it, we need to
make sense of the water as a dense medium. Simply
placing this duck on the surface helps the eye to interpret
the water for what it is, as well as adding visual interest to
the scene.

HOT TIP

Although we've
added a rippled
reflection in this
instance, in
many cases it's
enough just to
reduce the
opacity of the
water along the
flood line. Lower
the brush
opacity to
around 30%
and paint it out
on the layer
mask for an
instant
transparent
effect.

121

Getting the glazing bug

GLAZING EFFECTS are easy to create, and make the difference between an object looking like it's in a box and looking like it's inside a picture frame. The bug I've used here is in a three-dimensional box, but the technique works equally well for flat pictures in frames – or for windows, museum cases and other glazed surfaces.

Here, I've taken this bug box and added three different glazing effects to it, from simple glass to rippled plastic. The inset pictures show each effect in isolation against a black background, so it's easy to see how it works without the distraction of the main image getting in the way.

1 The simplest way to create a glass effect is simply to paint one on. Create a new layer behind the frame, and use a large soft-edged brush to add white bands. Set the opacity of the brush low – 10% or 20% – and

draw a series of diagonal white strokes. This can be a very subtle effect, and is most noticeable at the edges (where the glass meets the frame) rather than in the middle of the image. Build up the strokes as you go until the effect works. This is one of those occasions when a pressure-sensitive graphics tablet really comes into its own. The glass layer is shown here (inset), although obviously it makes more sense to draw it while viewing the full image.

2 To make the glass more convincing, consider adding a background image. Here, this shot of a room (inset) has been distorted slightly using the Wave filter: without the distortion it would look too flat and rigid. The opacity of this layer was then reduced to 10% so it was barely visible – after all, you don't want it to swamp the main image. The white bands used in the previous example were added over the top, their opacity reduced to 50%.

Any background image can be used; the choice depends largely on the supposed location of the object in question. For outdoor scenes, such as looking in through a window, a cloud reflection is particularly effective. Remember to keep the opacity low; if necessary, increase the contrast of the reflected image to make it more dramatic.

3 This version uses the Plastic Wrap filter to make the bug look like it's encased in polythene. First, a new layer was created and its mode set to Hard Light: this was filled with 50% gray, which is transparent in Hard Light mode. The brushstrokes (inset, top) were painted on using the Dodge and Burn tools to add highlight and shading to the image; the Plastic Wrap filter was applied (inset, bottom) to show the full effect. In

cases like this, it's worth applying the filter frequently as you paint to check the effect, which can be unpredictable; Undo after each time to carry on adjusting the background.

Glass: refraction

1 In this simple montage the glass vase, the table and the background are on three separate layers. The task is to make the background visible through the vase.

2 Begin by loading up the area taken up by the vase, by holding ⌘ ctrl and clicking on its thumbnail in the Layers palette. Then use the Elliptical Marquee tool, holding down ⌘ ⌥ ctrl alt to limit the area to just the bowl itself.

GLASS OBJECTS not only reflect what's around them, they also refract the view behind them. This refraction is easy to achieve; the trick to making the montage look real is to bring back the reflections in the original photograph so that they sit on top of the refracted image.

In this workthrough, we'll make this photograph of a glass vase look as if it's sitting within the scene, rather than simply stuck on top of it.

6 Now for the tricky bit – adding back the reflections from the original vase. Duplicate the vase layer, and delete the layer mask (without applying it). It will completely obscure the distorted background. Now choose Layer > Layer Style > Blending Options and drag the small black triangle under the This Layer slider (in the Blend If section) to the right. After a certain point, the vase will begin to turn transparent as all pixels darker than the position specified disappear.

3 Now hide the bowl layer, switch to the background and make a new layer from the selection using ⌘ J ctrl J.

4 Reselect the new layer by ⌘ ctrl clicking on its thumbnail in the Layers palette, and use the Spherize filter to create the refracted view. (If the bowl had been full of water, you'd need to flip this vertically to simulate the solid lens refraction.)

5 Turn on the vase layer so it's visible again, and create a layer mask. Using a large soft-edged brush, paint out the interior of the bowl so that the background becomes visible.

HOT TIP

Spherizing works well with spherical objects, as you'd expect. But if you want to distort the view seen through a cylinder, such as a glass wine bottle, you can still use the Spherize filter; this time, though, change the mode of the filter from Normal to Horizontal Only in the filter's dialog box.

7 Dragging the slider produces a hard cutoff as pixels darker than (in this case) 173 are hidden. That black slider is actually two sliders pinned together: to split them, hold down ⌥ alt and drag on the right half of the slider. When this is pulled all the way over to the right, any pixels whose brightness value are higher than 243 (in this instance) are fully visible; those pixels whose brightness values lie between the two sliders fade gradually from fully opaque to fully transparent.

Using Blending Options in this way to hide and show areas of a layer selectively is an extremely powerful tool: find out more about how it works in Chapter 2, Hiding and Showing.

As a final touch, the refracted background seen through the vase has been given a blue-green tint using the Color Balance dialog; I also painted out some of the stem on the layer mask to make it partially transparent.

SHORTCUTS
MAC WIN BOTH

Glass: reflection

CREATING REFLECTIONS in floors is easy to do, and can – with a little care – result in the kind of shiny, perfect reflection that looks like it was created in a 3D modeling program.

Here, we'll look at how to turn the dull floor we started off with into a highly reflective, polished surface.

1 This montage consists of two elements so far: the clouds and the grid floor. The first step is to adjust the color of the floor so that it more closely matches the colors of the sky.

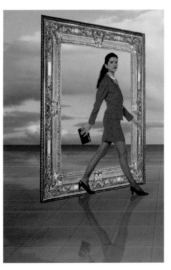

6 Adding this angled frame will present a different kind of reflection problem. First, though, we need to mask the woman's legs so that she's stepping through the frame.

2 The reflection of the sky in the floor is made by duplicating the sky layer, flipping it vertically and grouping it with the floor. With its opacity set to 30%, we can see the floor through it - but it looks rather dull.

7 Create a layer mask for the woman, and load the frame's area into it by holding ⌘ ctrl and clicking on the thumbnail; then hold ⌥ Shift alt Shift as you draw a marquee to limit the selection. Fill the mask selection with black to hide the leg.

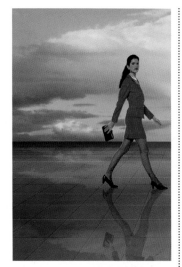

3 Changing the reflected sky's layer mode to Hard Light makes its reflection that much more punchy. This mode allows the light and dark in the underlying layer to show through, as in the highlights and shadows on the cracks.

4 This figure is walking parallel to the horizon, and so presents no problem when making the reflection. When the object to be reflected lies at an angle it gets more complicated, as we'll see later.

5 Once again, the reflected figure is lowered in opacity: this time, however, the reflection is set to Overlay mode, which produces a softer and less dramatic result.

HOT TIP

The technique shown here really only works for flat objects (such as the frame) or those parallel to the surface (the woman). To reflect more complex objects, you'll need to break them up into their component parts and distort each one individually. It can be done, but it's not a job for the faint-hearted.

  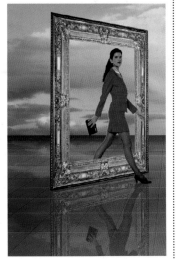

8 Simply flipping the frame to create its reflection clearly doesn't work: it ends up at completely the wrong angle. The solution is to use Free Transform to shear the reflection so that its top edge aligns with the bottom edge of the original frame.

9 To perform the shear, first use ⌘ T ctrl T to access Free Transform, then hold ⌘ Shift ctrl Shift while dragging a side handle (adding the Shift key constrains the movement to purely vertical).

10 Now we need to delete (or mask) those parts of the reflected frame and woman that intersect, in the same way as before. Also, the cloud reflection needs to be hidden behind the frame and woman reflections.

SHORTCUTS MAC WIN BOTH

127

Reflecting on fashion

1 Each element in this montage is on a separate layer – vital if we're going to make this sort of reflection work. The two Lens Flare effects were created on solid black layers set to Screen mode, so they could be moved around afterwards

WHEN THE GUARDIAN sent their science correspondent to review the Paris fashion shows (I still haven't worked out why) they needed a cover showing a scientist examining a catwalk model. Turning the catwalk from a simple surface into a shiny, reflective one made this illustration come alive.

As a footnote, the science correspondent decided he didn't want his image used in this way. Could I turn him around so we could only see the back of his head? With only 40 minutes left until the press deadline, it was impossible to start again – so the illustration was spiked. Sometimes even the most painstaking work ends up in the trash.

4 To create the reflections of the front row journalists, each one was copied and flipped individually, and arranged to follow the perspective; the overlap on each from the one in front was hidden with a layer mask.

2 The reflection of the row of lights up the side of the catwalk was created simply by duplicating the lights layer, moving it behind the lights and lowering the opacity. No need to flip them: one side of a disk is pretty much the same as the other.

3 The reflection of the model couldn't be simpler: I just flipped the original and lowered its opacity. But because the forward shoe was viewed from above in the original, I had to select that area in the reflection and nudge it down slightly.

5 One of the Lens Flare layers, flipped and grouped with the catwalk, adds useful random reflections to the otherwise plastic surface. At 30% opacity in Hard Light mode, the catwalk is still basically white.

6 The interest comes when that Lens Flare reflection is increased in strength to 70% opacity. Now, the catwalk surface takes on a burnished metal appearance, and looks altogether more appetizing.

HOT TIP

Sometimes you can simply flip an object to create its reflection; with a group, such as the front row of journalists set at an angle to the surface, you'll need to create the reflection of each one individually. Always keep those document layers intact!

129

Glass: putting it all together

NOW THAT WE'VE LOOKED at different ways of rendering glass, let's finish off this chapter by putting several of those elements together. Starting off with the simple montage above, we'll use the techniques covered in this chapter to glaze everything in sight.

To begin with, the bottle is only a shaped outline: we'll create this (as well as the rest of the glass) directly in Photoshop. The end result, on the opposite page, shows off our glazing efforts to their best advantage.

1 The first step is to glaze the window. This is achieved using the techniques discussed in the section Getting the Glazing Bug: first, a cloudscape is placed behind the window frame and set to 40% opacity, then, on a new layer, diagonal white brushstrokes are added to brighten the edges of the glazing. This technique is clearly a lot simpler if the window frame and the room interior are on separate layers.

The outline of the bottle is drawn with the Pen tool, and filled with mid gray.

Shading is added using Dodge and Burn tools to simulate lighting.

2 The bottle (below) was drawn using the Plastic Wrap technique explained in the section Miracle Wrap; the refractive effect was created using the method shown in the section Glass Refraction. Because this bottle is not spherical, the Spherizing of the background was performed in two stages - one for the neck, and one for the bowl. The steps used to draw the bottle are outlined below.

3 The table was drawn directly in Photoshop, using the Dodge and Burn tools to create the highlights. To make the surface transparent, that section was cut to a new layer and its opacity reduced. The reflections of the bottle and window in the table used the techniques described in the section Glass Reflections; the reflection in the greenhouse needed perspective distortion to achieve the correct angles.

HOT TIP

You can always photograph a bottle or glass rather than drawing it from scratch. The choice of background is critical: you need something bright enough for the glass to be visible, but must make sure the lighting doesn't cast shadows on it. It's also important to avoid reflections in the surface, unless you want to end up in your own montages.

Plastic Wrap adds the glass effect; with nothing reflected, it's unconvincing.

Increasing the contrast helps; the green color is added afterwards.

With the layer mask painted in, the refracted background becomes visible.

The original bottle is copied over the top, and Blending Options applied.

Photoshop Actions

THE ACTIONS PALETTE in Photoshop is a feature that most users tend to ignore, and when you look at the Actions shipped with the program it's hardly surprising. They allow you to perform such sequences as generating plastic-looking wood frames, creating dodgy reflections of type on water and filling the screen with molten lead. Which are hardly the sort of everyday tasks that make you want to explore the system further.

But Actions are capable of far more than building questionable special effects. At their basic level, Actions can be used simply to create keyboard shortcuts for tasks that would otherwise have you reaching for the menu bar. I've created Actions to bring up the Image Size dialog, the Canvas Size dialog and the Layers palette. I've also defined Actions to perform a Purge All command without asking me if I'm sure (of course I'm sure, that's why I chose it), to inverse the current selection (assigned to F1 – it only needs one hand, unlike Shift Command/Control I) and to turn a saved path into a selection. This last Action only works when the specified path is named Path 1; so I defined another Action to take the path I've just drawn, save it as Path 1, and then make it into a selection. That way, when I reopen the document I know I'll be able to load the path instantly.

Creating your own Actions is easy: simply choose New Action from the palette, choose a name and shortcut for it, then go ahead and act out the task you want it to do. Every step will be recorded as you go; at the end, press the Stop button and your Action will be saved. You can build in commands to make the Action pause for any variables you might need; and while you can't add menu choices while recording an Action in real time, you can add them afterwards by choosing Add Menu Item from the pop-up menu.

Actions can do far more, of course, than simply replicating menu commands. Among the Actions I use regularly are one to load a layer's transparency as a selection instead of having to Command/Control-click in the Layers palette – and this works even when the Layers palette is hidden.

Click here to build a 'stop' into the Action:
this one will simply open the Canvas Size
dialog, then wait for me to enter my figures

This is the Action name

Every step is detailed here

You can build an Action to
automate just about any sequence
of events. One task I perform
regularly is to delete a 1-pixel
edge around a cutout object,
which I find more satisfactory than either the Defringe or Remove White Matte
commands (see the section Losing the Edge in Chapter 1 for my reasons why).
This works as follows: first, the transparency of the layer is loaded up; then the
selection is contracted by 1 pixel, which was chosen from the Select/Modify
menu; then the selection is inversed, so everything else is selected; and then the
outside area is deleted. Finally, the selection edges are hidden so that I can see
if the result works: but it isn't deselected, so I can undo the deletion if I want to.
This is the Action shown above.

The most complex Action I use is to create new eyes for the celebrities and
politicians I use in my montages. I have to outline the eyes with the Pen tool
first, but then I simply press a key and the following sequence happens: a new
layer is created, named Eyeball, and the eye region filled with white. At this
point I've built a Stop feature into the Action, so that it asks me for the feather
radius I want to apply: I enter a value based on the size of the eyes in question.
The Action then continues, locking the transparency of the layer and inversing
the selection, then filling the feathered edge with an appropriate brown
shading; it then opens the file Eye (an image of a pupil), copies it and pastes it
into the document. This new layer is named Eye and is grouped with the
Eyeball layer so it only shows up where it overlaps it, and finally the mode of
the new layer is set to Multiply so that the shading on the Eyeball layer shows
through. And all this is accomplished in a few seconds.

One final word of advice: export your Actions (there's an option in the
palette) every time you modify them. Otherwise, if your computer crashes, you'll
lose the Action you've just defined.

7 Metal, wood and stone

HARD SURFACES are generally easier to simulate in Photoshop than those with transparency. Often, it's just a case of grouping a surface texture with the object you want to apply it to, and then adjusting the layer blending method so that the contours of the underlying object show through.

Reflective surfaces, such as metal, require special treatment: unlike wood or stone, you can't simply place a scan of a piece of metal on top. But the technique is easy to grasp and, once you get the hang of it, easy to reproduce.

In this chapter we'll also look at different ways of making lettering appear to be cast in the surface of a variety of materials.

Instant metal using Curves

1 Begin by opening the Curves dialog using ⌘ M ctrl M and click near the left-hand side of the diagonal line: drag vertically upwards

3 Now click again, further along the curve, and drag up again to make the high point for the next step. Once

THE SIMPLEST WAY to create an instant metallic effect is to use the Curves dialog. Metal differs from non-reflective surfaces in that it reflects the light in unpredictable ways: the light and shade aren't simply created by a single light source, but vary across the surface of the object.

We can simulate the effect of metal by drawing a stepped curve that reproduces the way metal reflects the light. On the following pages we'll look in more detail at how to get the best out of this technique; here, we'll simply turn this dull plastic monitor into a chrome-plated version.

5 Click further along the curve once more, and drag upwards to make the high point for the final step. At this

to make this steep curve. The image will appear very washed out at this stage, but it's just the initial step – it will all make sense later.

2 Now click a little further along the curve, and drag downwards as shown in the dialog. This will now make the image very much darker and

more contrasted. So far, we've created the first of what will become three peaks; we'll go on to build the other two to make the metallic effect work.

again the image will appear washed out: but the data is all still there, and we can continue to manipulate it.

4 Click further along, and drag down to complete the second step of our staircase. Now the image is beginning

to look far more shiny; but it still looks like it's made of plastic rather than metal.

HOT TIP

Using the Curves dialog to create metallic effects in this way can have unwanted results – in particular, it can create hard, pixelated lines around regions of high contrast on the original object. To remove these, use a small History brush to paint back the original image where it looks too harsh.

stage, we can begin to see the metallic effect taking shape, although the image still looks too bright.

6 Finally, click in the middle of the remaining part of the curve, and drag downwards. Now we've completed

the effect, and that dull metal monitor looks like it's made of gleaming chrome.

Metal using Adjustment Layers

1 This original Dalek model has been painted
using what the tin claimed was a metallic
paint. But when it was photographed, the result
looked dull and lifeless. We can use Curves again
to bring the shininess back.

CREATING METALLIC EFFECTS using the
Curves technique described on the
previous pages works fine, but gives us little
control over the result. It's far better to draw
the Curves on an Adjustment Layer: not only
can we mask and change the mode of the
effect, we can always go back and change the
shape of the curve at any time. Here, we'll use
this system to make our plastic Dalek look more
like the real thing.

4 As expected, the Curves effect has produced some harsh
pixellation. But because we applied it on an Adjustment
Layer, we can modify the target layer to fix the problem.
After locking the transparency of the Dalek using 🗍, apply
a small amount of Gaussian Blur – a 1 pixel radius maximum.

HOW TO **cheat** IN **Photoshop**

2 Create a new Curves Adjustment Layer by selecting it from the pop-up menu at the bottom of the Layers palette, and draw the same curve as we used on the previous pages. Here's the problem: the Curves effect has altered the color component as well, resulting in an ugly rainbow effect.

3 Because it's an Adjustment Layer, the problem is easily fixed. Simply change the layer mode (from the pop-up list at the top of the Layers palette) from Normal to Luminosity. Now, the Curves effect only affects the brightness and contrast of the underlying layer.

HOT TIP

The edges of layers can often look highly pixelated when a stepped Curves effect is applied. To get rid of this unwanted noise, simply group the Adjustment Layer with the target layer and most of the noise will disappear. Any extra noise can be painted out on the Adjustment Layer's mask.

5 Each Adjustment Layer comes with its own mask, which works precisely like a standard layer mask. We can use this to paint out the Curves effect on unwanted areas – the end of the suction cup, the orange light and the highlights in the black hemispheres on the Dalek's body.

6 The skirt still looked rather dull and lifeless. Easily remedied: we simply use the Burn tool to add a little shading to that area. Because we're looking through the Adjustment Layer, we can see the effect of the Curves as we paint with this tool.

SHORTCUTS

139

Metal with Lighting Effects

1 First make a new Alpha channel by clicking the icon at the bottom of the Channels palette. Since Lighting Effects only works in RGB, this will be Channel 4; its default name is Alpha 1. All the elements can be drawn directly on the channel, although you'd find it easier to create them as standard layers and then paste a merged copy into the channel afterwards. A faint application of the Clouds filter has been added to the background disc, as we'll see later.

THE LIGHTING EFFECTS FILTER is a useful tool for adding light and shade to an image: simply point the spotlights where you want them and adjust the settings. But the hidden function of Lighting Effects is its ability to use Alpha channels as bump maps to simulate three-dimensional images.

An Alpha channel is an additional channel (in addition to Red, Green and Blue) that Photoshop uses to store selection data. Some image libraries distribute CDs with their cutout information stored as Alpha channels rather than paths, because the channels can include transparency and fuzzy edges rather than just hard outlines.

The illustration above accompanied an article about the man who invented the mouse, for PC Pro magazine: the graphic border was produced using the method shown here.

4 Here's the result of applying the filter to our Alpha channel: those simple shapes and letterforms now look convincingly three-dimensional. Notice the difference in texture between the flat vertical bars and the background of the coin, to which the Clouds filter had been applied: this filter prevents large flat areas from looking too shiny and synthetic.

2 The next step is to blur the Alpha channel. This is necessary to prevent the final image showing hard edges around the contrasted elements; on the next page, we'll look in more detail at the effect of applying different amounts of blur to a bump map image. Now go back to the main RGB channels (you can use ⌘ ` *ctrl* `), create a new layer and fill the disc area with white – Lighting Effects won't work on an empty selection.

3 Open the Lighting Effects dialog, and specify the channel Alpha 1 from the Texture Channel pop-up list at the bottom of the dialog window. The default setting is White is High, which means that lighter areas will appear more raised than dark areas; I find it easier to work the other way around, so uncheck this box. Adjust the settings using the sliders until you get a clear effect with no burned-out hotspots.

5 Applying the same Curves technique as described on the previous pages brings out the shininess in our coin, making it look less like plastic and more like metal. That Clouds texture is also accentuated by the Curves process, giving the coin a pleasing battered effect.

6 Since the elements were all created as separate layers, it's easy to select them by holding ⌘ *ctrl* and clicking on each layer name in the Layers palette, holding *Shift* as well to add new layer outlines to the selection. Now the selected areas can be recolored using Color Balance (or any of the other color tools) to make our coin come to life.

HOT TIP

Lighting Effects only works on RGB images, so if you're working in CMYK you'll need to convert to RGB first. Even if you're creating a black and white illustration, you'll have to change it to RGB to use the filter, then change back to grayscale afterwards.

SHORTCUTS
MAC WIN BOTH

141

More on Lighting Effects

ALMOST ANY TEXTURE can be used as the basis for a Lighting Effects operation, as is shown here: Clouds and Noise are just two ways of generating natural-looking surfaces. Notice, as well, how the simple repeated screw heads shown in the final example produce an array of screws that are all lit slightly differently as their distance from the virtual light source varies.

The key to making artwork render well in Lighting Effects is to use just the right amount of blur on the Alpha channel that will be used as a texture map. So first, we'll look at how different amounts of blur affect the final appearance of the rendered artwork.

1 When no blur is added to the Alpha channel (above), the result after applying Lighting Effects (top) is harsh, with ragged, stepped edges.

2 Applying a 1-pixel radius Gaussian Blur to the Alpha channel softens the edges, and results in a far smoother image after Lighting Effects is applied.

6 The Clouds filter (above) produces a pleasingly random surface (top) when used as the basis of a Lighting Effects channel. It's a useful way to create an instant stone effect, which can be easily modified until it produces exactly the result you want.

7 Because the Alpha channel stores selections, we can press `⌥ ⌘ 4` `alt ctrl 4` to load up the lighter areas for us (top). We can now recolor them, then inverse the selection and recolor the rest to create a more dynamic effect (above).

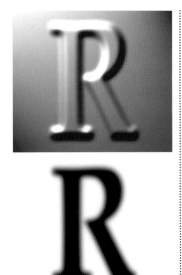

3 The greater the amount of blur, the more raised the result will be. Here, a 2-pixel blur results in a significantly taller object.

4 Increasing the blur to 4 pixels produces a result in which the edges thicken too much: this looks like it was cast from an old mold.

5 An 8-pixel blur is clearly a blur too far: Lighting Effects has trouble making sense of this, and the result is merely fuzzy.

8 Even the tiniest variations in shade can have dramatic effects. The 2% Gaussian Noise (above) is too faint to be seen clearly here; but the result (top) is a grainy, textured surface.

9 Increasing the Gaussian Noise amount to 20% produces a far more striking result: here, we've produced a rough, stony surface in just a few seconds using this technique.

10 The screws around this perimeter were created by dabbing a soft brush once, then drawing a diagonal line across it. Because the letter M is brighter than the background, it appears to be recessed rather than raised.

HOT TIP

If you're not sure how much blur or noise to apply, try copying the base artwork and pasting it into several new Alpha channels. Then, when you open the Lighting Effects dialog, you'll be able to choose between them from the pop-up list to see which one produces the results you want.

SHORTCUTS
MAC | WIN | BOTH

Rust, grime and decay

S O FAR, WE'VE LOOKED at ways of using Lighting Effects to make bright, shiny objects. But it can just as easily make metal surfaces that look as if they've been knocking around for a few years. Making objects appear to be old and used can greatly add to the realism of an illustration.

Starting with this simple sign, above, we'll run Lighting Effects a couple of times and hopefully end up with something that looks like it belongs in the real world.

1 The first step, as always, is to blur the artwork after it's made into a new channel. Because our sign is supposed to be pressed out of a sheet of metal, we don't want too much variation in height: there are basically just two shades here, black and white.

4 Now we'll return to our Alpha channel, and add some noise to it. This will form the basis for the rust, but we don't need a lot of noise: as ever, a small change in a channel makes a huge difference when Lighting Effects is applied. Here, a Gaussian Noise amount of 6 has been used.

2 Here's the result of applying the Lighting Effects filter after the previous artwork was saved as a channel. So far, it looks more like plastic than metal; but since we want it to look painted rather than polished, we won't apply the Curves as in the previous examples.

3 Because the channel that Lighting Effects used can also store selections, we can press ⌥ ⌘ 4 / alt ctrl 4 to load up the white areas as a selection. This is tinted using Hue/Saturation; the selection is then inversed using ⌘ Shift I / ctrl Shift I and the raised areas brightened up.

5 On a new layer, the Lighting Effects filter is applied again. This time the result is tinted brown, once again using the Hue/Saturation dialog. There's no need to load up specific areas using the channels: we want to tint the entire image.

6 Now it's just a matter of making a layer mask for the new brown layer, and painting it out selectively to reveal the original sign beneath. After using the Brush tool to paint out large areas, turn to the Smudge tool to fine-tune the result by smudging streaks of rust into the mask.

HOT TIP

If you don't want your rust to look as extreme as this example, stop after step 3 and create a new layer, set to Hard Light mode and grouped with the sign layer. You can now paint on this layer using oranges and browns to create rust-like shading on the layer beneath.

SHORTCUTS

MAC WIN BOTH

Metal embossing made easy

1 Here's the original bottle, complete with plastic tube. It would have been hugely difficult to erase the tube without damaging the logo; so I ignored the logo.

2 The tube and logo were both cloned out, and the overall contrast increased to make the bottle more appealing. I also added a slight red tint to the perfume inside.

W HEN PERFUME company Amouage wanted a new series of advertisements for their products, they had all the bottles photographed in a studio. But the photographer couldn't get the plastic tube out of the bottle without breaking the bottle; so I had to remove it in Photoshop.

To get the metallic effect on the logo, I used the plug-in filter EyeCandy 4000, which produces gleaming chrome. You can read more about this innovative and useful tool in Chapter 11, Carry on Spending.

6 The original logo was gold leaf placed onto molded glass, so I had to reproduce that effect too. The logo area was enlarged by a few pixels, smoothed and made into a new layer, then embossed using Layer Effects.

7 When the gold was put back into position, I was able to reduce the opacity of the glass embossing from its original rather overstated appearance to something that would look more plausible.

3 I redrew the Amouage logo in Illustrator, using some flat artwork as a template. Of course, I only needed to redraw one half; the other was made simply by mirroring the first.

4 This logo was then brought into Photoshop, and the EyeCandy 4000 Chrome filter was applied to get the shiny effect. It's the fastest way of making shiny metal that I know of.

5 The logo was distorted on the bottle to fit the viewing angle of the original logo, and tinted so that it matched the color of the shiny gold lid of the bottle.

HOT TIP

If there's one lesson to be learnt from this example, it's that you don't always have to do things the obvious way. I spent a long time trying unsuccessfully to remove the tube from around the logo before I realized that I could simply replace the logo. The object was to produce a beautiful and appealing image, rather than to show photographic truth.

8 Although the bottles had been photographed from several angles, I didn't want to have to go through the clean-up process for each one. So I split the bottle into three components, and distorted each separately.

9 Matching the new perspectives of the front and side of the bottle was easier than might have been expected: the reflections and refractions in the glass worked even when distorted.

10 The only element I took from the other photographs was the lid: it would have been almost impossible to make the existing lid fit the new perspective, given its complex geometry.

147

Reflection on a knife edge

1 The knife blade and the handle were first drawn as two separate layers, using the Pen tool to create the outlines. The hole in the blade was made with the Elliptical Marquee.

THE MOST ABSTRACT CONCEPTS are often the hardest ones to illustrate. This illustration for the Sunday Telegraph was commissioned to accompany a feature on how directors of top companies were facing pay cuts. Rather than going down the obvious, cartoony route of showing a miserable exec pulling out his empty pockets, the art editor came up with this idea of a sushi knife slicing through a pile of banknotes.

The property that makes flat metal look metallic is the reflections seen in it: but here, I didn't want any extraneous elements to confuse the issue. So the effect had to be created simply using light and shade, with only the copied banknotes making the reflection element.

4 After increasing the contrast on the blade, I selected a band at the bottom with the Lasso tool and added strong shading with Dodge and Burn to make the knife edge.

7 The banknotes were stacked up and shaded using the techniques shown in the Lock and Load section of Chapter 1, Natural Selection.

2 Basic shading was added using the Dodge and Burn tools; the strong diagonal slant gives the impression of light on a reflecting surface.

3 The blade selection was loaded up by ⌘ *ctrl* clicking on the layer name, and then nudged down and to the right; the inverse was shaded using Dodge and Burn again.

5 A new layer was filled with white, grouped with the blade and set to Multiply. The Noise filter was followed by vertical Motion Blur to make the brushed steel effect.

6 The first of the banknotes was simply distorted using Free Transform so that it lay in a convincing perspective across the knife blade.

8 The top banknote was cut in half, stepped up, and the process repeated each side of the blade: an additional couple of notes were distorted to fly up from the pile.

9 Copies of the top note and the sides were flipped and distorted and then grouped with the blade, and their opacity lowered so that they looked like dull reflections.

HOT TIP

The hardest part of creating this image was making the reflection of the topmost banknote marry correctly with the original: because the note had been distorted, it was difficult to handle the reflection. The solution was to cheat: different sections of the reflection were distorted separately, so that the key elements matched those in the original note.

SHORTCUTS
MAC WIN BOTH

The art of wood turning

1 This plinth has been created using Adobe Dimensions, and imported into Photoshop, For more about that program see Chapter 9: The Third Dimension.

2 A scan of a piece of wood is placed on top of the plinth layer, and grouped with it by pressing ⌘ G ctrl G or by clicking the line between the layers in the Layers palette.

ALMOST ANY OBJECT can be turned into wood simply by wrapping a piece of wood around it and changing the layer mode so the original object shows through. Unlike other textures, though, wood has a grain which needs to follow the contours of the base object. To see how the bust was made, see The Philosopher's Stone later in this chapter.

6 A new section of wood is taken using a circular selection, which is then rotated 90° and Spherized to make it wrap around the base better. The circle is then squeezed to make this ellipse, which fits the base dimensions.

7 This base section of wood is then grouped with the plinth layer, and a new layer mask is added. We don't need to draw the mask again: simply duplicate and invert the mask that was created for the column layer.

3 Now we need to make the base layer show through, by changing the layer mode using the pop-up menu at the top of the Layers palette. This is Multiply: it's far too dark.

4 Changing the layer mode to Overlay produces a far better result. We can clearly see all the contours of the underlying object, while maintaining the wood texture.

5 Having the wood grain running vertically is fine for the column, but looks wrong on the capital and base. Using the Pen tool, I've created a layer mask to hide the top and bottom.

8 Once again, we set the mode of this layer to Overlay. The Spherized wood now fits the shape of the base perfectly; and because we inverted the column's layer mask, the two match together without a visible join.

9 To make the capital, we simply duplicate the base layer and then unchain the link between the layer and its mask. We can then drag the wood ellipse up into place, and the layer mask is already there for us.

10 All that's needed now is to add a little extra shading beneath the capital, and around the far side of the base of the plinth. This is painted directly onto the underlying plinth layer using the Burn tool.

HOT TIP

Although we set the layer mode of the wood layer to Overlay in this instance, it won't suit all purposes; it all depends on the characteristics of the base layer, and the texture and grain of the wood you're using. Try Hard Light and Soft Light, as well as Multiply, to see which produces the best effect for your artwork.

SHORTCUTS
MAC WIN BOTH

151

Making a better impression

1 This may be an accurate representation of the Presidential Seal, but as it stands it's hardly a beautiful object in its own right. Let's take this flat artwork and make it a little more attractive.

W E CAN USE THE TEXTURE of a wooden surface as the base for any artwork, turning a two-dimensional design into one that looks as if it's been carved in wood. In the example above, I've used the complex outlines of this coat of arms to create a solid-looking object. The original design for this crest was in black and white, so the embossing has to do all the work.

The Seal of the President of the United States, by contrast, has no interest in its outline – it's simply a round disk. Unlike the crest, it does have the advantage of color to create more interest, and we can make use of this.

4 Now that the seal detail is in our Alpha channel, we can load it as a selection using ⌘⌥4 ctrl alt 4 ; the brighter areas will be more fully selected than the dark areas. Returning to the wooden disk, we can now make a new layer from that selection using ⌘J ctrl J . This layer will appear with the bevel from the disk applied: as it stands, it's far too blobby.

2 To begin, we'll take the same piece of wood as we used in the previous example. After stretching it so it covers the seal, hold ⌘ ctrl and click on the seal's name in the Layers palette to load up its selection; then inverse the selection using ⌘ Shift I ctrl Shift I and delete the outside. The bevel is applied using Layer Effects, with a 15-pixel bevel to give the disk a sense of three-dimensionality.

3 Now we're going to turn the original seal into a selection. Copy it, then make a new channel by clicking on the icon at the bottom of the Channels palette; then paste the copy in place, where it will appear in black and white. This can now be used as a workable selection.

HOT TIP

When copying a layer into a new alpha channel, it's important to make sure the copied version appears in exactly the same position as the original. The easiest way is to hold ⌘ ctrl and click on the layer's name to select its outlines; then copy, and with the outlines still selected, paste onto a new channel. This method will ensure the positioning is precise.

5 Double-click the layer effect in the Layers palette to open the dialog, and change the numbers. Here I've increased the depth from the default 100% to 200% to make it stronger; but I've also reduced the bevel size to just three pixels, so that the detail remains crisp. Some of the detail has failed to appear after the selection process, such as the wings of the eagle; but the next step will fix that.

6 Finally, move the original seal layer to the top. We need to change its layer mode so that the wood and beveling show through. Once again, we have a choice of layer modes open to us: although Overlay worked on the example on the previous page, it's too strong here. Instead, I've opted for Soft Light, which brings back much of the original color while retaining the subdued sense of stained wood.

SHORTCUTS
MAC WIN BOTH

153

Timber floors with varnish

1 To turn this piece of wood into a floor, the first step is to mark out the planks. It's easiest to draw a rectangular selection in QuickMask and fill it, then copy it across: that way you can be sure they're all the same size.

2 Make a new layer from the selection. I've used the Bevel section of Layer Styles to add the shading lines. Be sure to keep the Highlight value fairly low, or you'll find it too glaring when the floor is finished.

I HAVE A CONFESSION to make: I only have one piece of wood. At least, there's only one piece I tend to use for all my wooden needs: it's this image of the back of an old pencil box I scanned in 1989. You can still see the screw holes that held the base to the sides – it wasn't even a particularly sophisticated pencil box. The point is, though, that you really don't need a lumber yard full of different types of wood; as long as the piece you're using has a strong enough grain, it can be put to most purposes fairly well.

6 Adding the nails is optional, but can help with the sense of flooring. On a new layer, make a small circular selection, fill with a mid grey and add a little shading to it; then duplicate three times (you can see the nails on the fifth plank from the left).

7 Copy that group of nails to all the other wood joins by holding ⌥ *alt* as you drag with the Move tool. Be sure to hold the mouse down within the nail area before dragging, or you'll create a new layer each time you drag. Finally, merge all the layers.

3 Now inverse the selection, and make a new layer from the wood base: apply the same beveling by dragging the layer effect from the previous layer onto this one. Finally, flip the new layer vertically so the grain lines don't match up.

4 Split one set of floorboards into irregular lengths by making rectangular selections, and make another new layer using ⌘ J *ctrl* J; the bevel will automatically be applied to the new layer.

5 Repeat the process for the other set of planks, and adjust the brightness of both to make more irregularity in the planks.

HOT TIP

Applying a perspective distortion to the wood necessarily makes it narrower at the top than at the bottom. If your target image is wider than the original wood flooring, duplicate the layer and move it horizontally so the two overlap by about an inch; then make a layer mask to blur the join lines and merge the two layers to make a floor that's nearly twice as wide.

 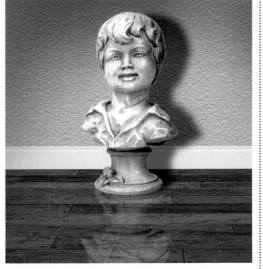

8 Your floor is now ready to be inserted in whatever document you want. Use Free Transform to make it fit the space: hold down ⌘ ⌥ *Shift* *ctrl* *alt* *Shift* while dragging one of the top corner handles to create the perspective distortion. A floor like this can be made to fit in just about any space you want to fill. This wall, incidentally, was easily made using the Texturizer filter.

9 With the shading in place, the floor looks very much more realistic. Applying the varnish is far less messy than working with the real thing: simply make a reflected copy of whatever object you're placing on the floor, and set its Layer mode to Soft Light for that glossy appearance. For more on how to achieve this effect, see the reflection sections in Chapter 6, Shiny Surfaces.

SHORTCUTS
MAC WIN BOTH

The philosopher's stone

1 Choosing the original photograph was the key to the success of this project. I immediately rejected one that showed the philosopher smiling: the ancient Greeks never bared their teeth. This image showed the right sort of side lighting, without any strong shadows.

2 The first step was to cut out the head, and knock out the color using the Desaturate command ⌘ *Shift* U *ctrl* *Shift* U. I then copied a section of his forehead to get a suitable shade and texture, stretched it and cut it to the shape of his neck and shoulders.

W HEN THE INDEPENDENT newspaper wanted to run an article comparing ancient and modern philosphers, they had busts of the ancient Greeks – but only a photograph of contemporary philosopher Alain de Boton. It seemed like a good idea to turn him into stone to match his predecessors, and achieving the task in Photoshop was obviously going to be quicker and cheaper than finding a sculptor who could reproduce his likeness in marble in time for a 5pm deadline.

6 The pupils were painted in by making elliptical selections within the eyes, and using the Dodge and Burn tools once again to make them look recessed. Care was taken here to make the shading match the surrounding area as closely as possible – the shading had to be kept subtle.

7 This scan of a chunk of marble would add both texture and color to our bust. Because the head and shoulders are two layers, I couldn't simply group the marble with the base; instead, I made a layer mask encompassing both the underlying layers.

3 Carved hair is very different from the real thing, so I took another section of forehead and this time shaped it to cover the hair and eyebrows of the original. I also patched the forehead using the Clone tool to hide the stray hairs there.

4 Adding shading using the Dodge and Burn tools made the hair look carved in stone: I also added muscle lines to the neck. Remember you can temporarily access the Dodge tool while using Burn by holding ⌥ *alt* as you paint.

5 The eyes also needed painting out, again by cloning texture from the forehead; shading was added afterwards to make them look more three-dimensional. I also cloned over the lips at a low opacity to tone them down slightly.

8 Multiply, Hard Light, Overlay and Soft Light modes would all have allowed the image to show through the marble. The choice is determined by each instance; in the end I chose Soft Light, reducing the opacity to 70% so that the strong texture in the marble didn't swamp the image.

9 To strengthen the whole image, I made a new Adjustment Layer and increased the Contrast while reducing the Brightness. Adjustment Layers have the advantage of being editable later, which meant I could always remove it if it needed altering or wasn't working.

10 Although I wanted the bust to look like pale marble, it's just as easy to make it appear to be modeled out of granite or any darker material. Here, I've taken the same piece of marble and changed its mode to Multiply to get an altogether stronger effect.

SHORTCUTS
MAC WIN BOTH

157

Carving in stone

1 This piece of stone is nicely mossy at the bottom, and will do perfectly as the basis for our grave. I tend to carry my digital camera with me whenever I'm likely to stumble upon an interesting building or texture.

THIS ILLUSTRATION WAS FOR THE COVER of the Sunday Times Magazine. The shape of the plinth was modeled in Dimensions (see Chapter 9), and the stone texture wrapped around it. The pigeon perched on the top is simply there to add a sense of scale.

Carving text in stone is now easier than ever, thanks to the Emboss feature in Layer Effects. Here, we'll look at how to make a gravestone from scratch, in just a few simple steps.

4 After creating your text, render it into a layer and then distort it using Free Transform to match the perspective of the tombstone. This text is loaded as a selection by ⌘ *ctrl* clicking on its name in the Layers palette, and the selection made into a new layer from the stone layer.

2 Because we want this grave to be somewhat rough around the edges, draw the outline using the Lasso tool to get the unevenness that couldn't be achieved with the Pen tool. This selection can then be made into a new layer using ⌘ J ctrl J.

3 The same selection is copied from a different part of the original stone material, and offset to make the edge. Shading can be added using the Dodge and Burn tools, making it darker on the undersides of the edge, and lighter on the upper faces.

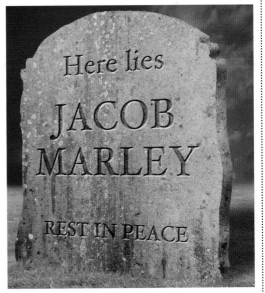

5 After darkening the stone lettering slightly to make it stand out better, use Layer Effects to create the carved effect. Use Emboss rather than Bevel for this, as it makes a more convincing carved effect; remember to set the position to be Down rather than Up, so it's lit from above.

6 When the background is added, it's simply a matter of blending the stone into its surroundings. Darken the edge slightly, and add a shadow on the grass behind it; the grass is brought in front of the base of the stone using the technique described in the Chapter 2, Hiding and Showing.

HOT TIP

Choose an appropriate typeface for your lettering to make the whole effect more convincing. Sans serif lettering is virtually never used on graves, for good reason: it's the serifs that are carved first, and which prevent the stone from splitting as the thick letters are incised. This is, in fact, the reason why the ancients invented serif lettering in the first place.

SHORTCUTS
MAC WIN BOTH

The point of illustration

BRIEFS FOR ILLUSTRATIONS come in three basic varieties. There are those who will send you the copy for the article in question, and wait for you to come up with a visual idea to accompany it. There are art editors who will work out the idea on their own, get it passed by the editor, and sometimes even supply a rough sketch of what they want. And finally there are editors themselves, who will insist on the first idea that pops into their heads and expect it to be turned into a work of art.

I have nothing against newspaper editors. Many of them are charming individuals who are great conversationalists and probably make outstanding parents. But they frequently lack the ability to think in visual terms. One of the illustrations I'm frequently asked to create is a montage showing a politician taking money out of someone's pocket (this usually happens around budget time). I pause, take a deep breath and explain patiently that the problem is that newsprint technology has yet to embrace the wonders of animation. There's no difference, in a still image, between a politician taking money out of someone's pocket and putting money into it. This has to be explained with great tact, of course, since ultimately these are the people who pay for my children's overpriced trainers.

It comes down to a question of what's desirable, what's visually interesting and what's humanly possible. The purpose of an illustration in a magazine or newspaper is to draw the reader into the piece and to make them want to read the article to which it's attached. It should express the sense of the article without giving away the punchline, and without prejudging the issue (that's best left to the journalist who wrote the story). An illustration in a printed publication is not a work of art; it's an advertisement for the story, and its job is to sell the story to the reader. Sometimes – at the best of times – it can be a work overflowing with artistic integrity and perfect composition. But if it doesn't relate to the story in question (and make that story seem interesting) then it's failed to do its job.

Those taking up photomontage for the first time frequently fall into the trap of piling on evocative imagery in the hope that the result will be poignant. I've seen student artwork that incorporates a baby, a flaming pile of dollar bills, a nuclear explosion and a McDonald's wrapper within one image. Look, they say, all human life is here: it must mean something. But this is the visual equivalent of Tchaikovsky's 1812 overture with added reverb and a drum'n'bass backing: the cacophony simply prevents us from seeing the issues.

Labeling, above all, is to be avoided at all costs. The days when you could depict Uncle Sam wearing a hat with Government printed on it rowing a boat labeled Economy while tipping out a handful of urchins labeled Unemployed rightfully died out in the early nineteenth century – and yet illustrators are still asked to label their artwork today. I nearly always refuse, unless the wording can be incorporated into the image in a meaningful way. The destruction of a building bearing the sign Internet Hotel seems, to me, to be a reasonable request; the sinking of a boat labeled Fair Deal does not.

When you execute an original idea successfully, you can confidently expect to be asked to reproduce it within a few months. I've drawn cakes for the 20th birthday of Channel 4, the 10th birthday of Sky television, the carving up of Channel 4 and the first birthday of satellite channel E4 – all for the same newspaper. I've blown up computers, telephones, televisions and video recorders, and I've tattered the flags of at least half a dozen of the world's top blue-chip companies. And I've completely lost count of the number of company logos I've pasted onto the backs of poker cards.

The hard part is keeping each new version as fresh as the first. I've often made the mistake of assuming that readers will find the repetition of the same idea tedious: but it is a folly, for the stark truth is that readers of publications cast barely a glance at the image that an illustrator has sweated blood over. Illustration, for the most part, is simply the ephemeral wrapping that's discarded once it's done its job.

8 Paper and fabric

IN THE LAST CHAPTER we looked at hard surfaces – metal, wood and stone. Paper and fabric, by contrast, are floppy, malleable substances that bend, crease and crumple. It's getting these creases and wrinkles right that's the key to making paper look like it's really made of paper, and that includes banknotes as well as letters and documents.

The fabric section of this chapter covers clothes, flags and banners; all the objects that hang or flutter in an irregular manner. We'll examine the easiest way to make a flat, PostScript drawing of a flag look like the real thing fluttering in the breeze, using simple shading techniques combined with distortion filters.

How to make a load of money

SCANNING BANKNOTES is easy: you just lay them on a flatbed scanner (but watch out for copyright – some governments take a dim view of reproducing their currency). Making them look like they exist in the real world takes a little bit more effort.

To add more interest and realism to banknotes, we can use the Shear filter to give them a bit of a twist. This useful filter makes objects ripple convincingly, adding a pleasing third dimension to otherwise flat artwork; when appropriate shading is added, a single banknote can be made to look like a whole pile of separate notes. Here, we'll work on a 500 Euro note.

1 The Shear filter only works horizontally, so before you apply it you need to rotate the artwork by 90°. Increase the Canvas Size, if necessary, to allow extra space at the sides for the image to distort into.

2 When you first open the Shear dialog, you'll see a straight line. Click in the middle of this line and you'll create an anchor point: drag this point, and you'll make a smooth curve that precisely bends the artwork.

5 Repeating the Shear filter with different settings can make the dollar bill ripple in different ways. Here, two different applications of the filter show how the same bill can be distorted into different forms. The Shear filter is far more controllable than the Wave filter, as it allows us to draw precisely the curve we want; and the preview's large enough to see.

3 If you're working on an element within a larger montage, draw a marquee selection that encompasses the layer you want to work on, so the Shear filter only affects that area of the artwork.

4 Shading added to the result, using the Burn tool, gives the sense of the sheared object being truly three-dimensional. Rather like those gestalt optical illusions, you can choose to see the image in one of two ways. The eye will interpret shaded areas as being recessed, and unshaded areas raised: so in the top example above, the raised ripple is on the left; in the lower example, it appears to be on the right. In fact, it's the same bill both times.

HOT TIP

You don't need to apply the Shear tool separately for every banknote in a pile: three or four sheared versions are usually sufficient. Distorting the notes using Free Transform will be enough to make them all look different. When you combine several notes in one montage, add shading using the Burn tool to enhance the effect.

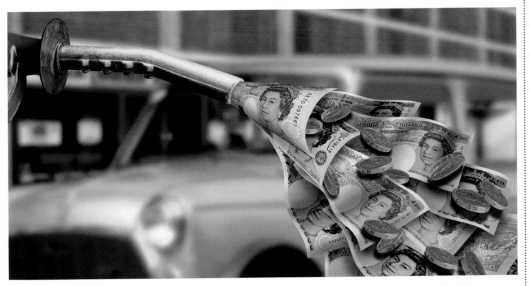

6 This illustration for the Sunday Telegraph was to accompany an article about the increased cost of motoring following a rise in the price of crude oil. The banknotes were all distorted using the Shear tool, as described here: those coming directly out of the pump's spout were also sheared horizontally. Each note was then distorted using Free Transform to achieve a sense of perspective, and shading was added beneath each note to make it stand out from the note below. Adding the coins simply made the result look more dynamic.

Judging a book by its cover

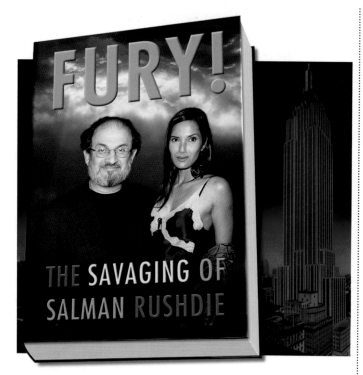

FURY!
THE SAVAGING OF SALMAN RUSHDIE

WHEN AUTHOR SALMAN RUSHDIE visited New York, he expected to be fêted: instead, he was slated. For the story about his mishap in The Independent, I was asked to produce a book cover showing the headline for the article, in the style of Rushdie's latest volume.

But hardback books are hard objects to photograph. Apart from the problem of getting the right angle, the close trimming of the paper makes it look like a solid block rather than individual pages: so there was no option but to draw the book from scratch. And here's how it was done.

1 The paper is created in the same way as the cards were stacked up in Chapter 4. The difference here, of course, is that the pages are stacked neatly rather than randomly: select a shadowed page and then nudge it up and left a couple of times with the cursor keys, holding ⌘ *alt* to make the copies.

SHOWBIZ!
How I sold my soul but kept my promises
Marianne de Vorce

4 A copy of the cover is made, moved behind it and filled with a dark blue. This is the edge of the board beneath the paper wrapper: it's only just visible, but it makes the difference between a paperback and a hardback. We'll use a similar technique for creating the back cover.

2 The cover is assembled using as many layers as required; these are linked and made into a new Layer Set. Duplicate this set and merge its contents; then distort the resulting composite layer to fit the shape of the book cover. The reason for this seemingly tortuous route is that the original cover is kept intact, so changes can be made later.

3 Shading on the edges of the cover helps to make it look as if it wraps around the hard boards. Using the Burn tool, click just above a corner, then hold *Shift* and click at the bottom of the same edge. A burn line will be drawn as a straight line between the two click points.

5 Now for the shadow of the cover cast on the pages. It's worth creating this as a separate layer, grouped with the paper layer: paint straight lines with the Brush tool, set to a low opacity, in the same manner as outlined for the Burn tool in step 3 above.

6 The final elements are added to complete the book: the back cover, the spine, and the flaps that tuck beneath the board covers. I've also added some general shading to the cover using the Dodge and Burn tools to prevent it looking too flat and two-dimensional.

HOT TIP

Creating the cover as a separate element is the best way to build a book such as this. Sometimes, though, you don't know one element, such as the title, before you start. To make it easy to align new text and objects to the same perspective, first make a simple grid and distort it to fit the cover; then it's easy to align the new objects with that grid, which can be hidden afterwards.

SHORTCUTS
MAC WIN BOTH

167

Paper: folding and crumpling

WHEN ART EDITORS are stuck for a visual idea, they fall back on a piece of paper with the concept written on it. An executive might hold a paper entitled Restructuring Proposal; a real estate agent might wield one with the word Contract emblazoned on it in red ink.

Whatever the wording on the paper, the last thing you want to do is to leave it as a flat sheet. Simply distorting it into perspective is rarely sufficient: this is paper, after all, and not a sheet of plastic; it bends, creases and deforms as it's handled.

Here, we'll look at a couple of different paper treatments: a simple fold, and the crumpled effect seen on a piece of paper that's been stuffed in a back pocket for too long.

1 Here's the business letter we'll use in both our examples. If you're going to use a letter, you'll obviously need some text on it. It doesn't usually matter what this is, as long as it doesn't begin Lorem Ipsum: readers may not recognize the fake Latin text, but the person who commissioned you certainly will.

2 Select just the top half of the letter and apply the Shear filter to it, using the technique described earlier in this chapter. When working on the top half of the paper, be sure not to move the anchor point at the bottom of the dialog box or the two halves will no longer match up.

6 To begin the Crumple effect, we'll use the Wave filter to distort the basic letter. This can be a confusing filter at first glance, because there appear to be so many variables: but it's quite controllable. The number of Generators determines the different number of waves; set to 1, the effect will be too regular and phoney. Because we want long, sweeping curves, raise the Wavelength levels: the higher the levels, the greater the length of each wave. You can use the Amplitude sliders to determine the wave height, but you'll get far more control by simply lowering the horizontal and vertical scale to make the wave effect less extreme.

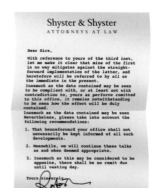

3 After applying the filter, leave the top half of the paper selected and use the Burn tool with a large, soft-edged brush to add gentle shading above the crease line. Add a little more where the paper turns away at the top top give the impression of it bending over away from us.

4 Now select the bottom half of the paper, and apply the Shear filter again. You'll need to click the Defaults button to reset the tool to a vertical line; you can then add whatever distortions you want.

5 Now, with the bottom half distorted as well, add some shading to that half of the paper, again without deselecting it. you can also add a little shading elsewhere on the paper to give the sense of a gentle ripple.

7 Now use the Lasso tool to make irregular vertical selections. Don't make the lines dead straight: hold the ⌥ alt key and click points at intervals along the letter to make the tool draw straight selection lines between each point you click.

8 Now use a large, soft brush with the Burn tool to add the shading. Keep the brush on the deselected side of the selection line, so that only the edge of the brush has an effect on the paper. Don't paint exactly along the lines, but fade off away from the edges for an altogether more realistic appearance.

9 Now deselect, and use the Lasso tool once more to make a series of horizontal selections. Use the Burn tool once more to add the new shading within the selected area, once again being careful not to overdo the effect.

HOT TIP

Although real paper tends to be white, you'll have a hard time working on it if you leave it pure white. Lower the white point of your paper using Curves or Levels to just take the edge off the brightness, and you'll find it far easier to see what you're doing. You can always paint highlights back in later if you need to.

SHORTCUTS
MAC WIN BOTH

169

Folds and wrinkles

1 The original artwork was created on a rectangular banner, and the text layers were merged into it. This banner was then rotated and curved slightly using the Shear tool (see earlier in this chapter); Free Transform was then used to make the bottom corners fall together slightly.

FABRIC NEVER HANGS STRAIGHT. It's the folds, creases and wrinkles that give it its distinctive quality. But it's an appearance that's surprisingly easy to reproduce in Photoshop.

Glancing at the composite image above, you might think that the lettering had been distorted using some complex system to make it follow the fold lines in the banner. In fact, the only distortion on the text comes from the initial shearing and perspective applied to the whole banner: the illusion of rippling text is created entirely by the play of light and shade across it.

4 Now for the shading. Use the Burn tool, and choose a medium sized, soft-edged brush. Lower the opacity to between 20% and 40% so the effect isn't too strong, and paint a shallow curve running from corner to corner, dipping into the banner.

7 Hold the ⌥ alt key again to use the Dodge tool, and paint another highlight above that shadow. It may take a few attempts before you're able to paint the Dodge strokes in the right way; if you make a mistake, just Undo and try it again.

2 To add the texture, the Texturizer filter was used with the Canvas setting. It's a simple way to make smooth, flat artwork look more natural. Any grayscale document can be used to generate the textures used by this filter, so you can define your own easily.

3 The result of the Texturizer filter was too strong, so we'll reduce its effect. Rather than going through the dialog again, there's a simpler way: after applying this (or any) filter, use the Fade menu option (Edit menu) to reduce the opacity. Here, it's been taken down to 30% of its original strength.

5 Now hold the ⌥ *alt* key to get the Dodge tool and paint a parallel curve directly above the one you just drew. This will brighten the artwork, where the Burn tool darkened it: used together, the effect will be of a highlight above and a shadow below the fold.

6 Using the Burn tool again, paint a second curve below the first, again running roughly from corner to corner. It really helps to use a pressure-sensitive graphics tablet for a job like this, but it can be done with the mouse – just use a lower opacity and build up each shadow.

8 Continue in the same fashion until you've made a series of curves running right to the bottom of the banner. The flat artwork we started with now looks more like a piece of fabric that's hanging from its corners.

9 To finish off, add more folds in the corners of the banner. These won't reach right to the corners, but follow the same lines to make the edges of the banner look more realistic. Now's also a good time to strengthen those highlights and shadows that don't show up well enough.

HOT TIP

Using the Texturizer filter to add the canvas texture to fabric can result in a blocky, repetitive tiled pattern. If you have a digital camera, it's worth instead photographing a piece of real canvas (the back of an oil painting works well) and simply overlaying that on top of your artwork using Hard Light or Multiply mode, and a low opacity.

SHORTCUTS
MAC WIN BOTH

171

Ripping and tearing

1 The initial poster was created using text distortion to bend the lettering; the figure was stylized using the Watercolor filter. As it stands, it's a brash image that looks nothing like a real poster.

THE POSTERS IN THE ILLUSTRATION ABOVE, created for .net magazine, needed just a little distressing to make them look more realistic. Here, we'll take the process several steps further to turn this flat, artificial poster into something that looks as if it's been hanging around on the wall for a long time.

In most cases, you wouldn't want to add this much destruction to a single poster – I've gone to rather extreme lengths to illustrate the techniques involved. Often, only the smallest amount of shading is required to make a poster convincing: in the illustration above, the Internet Toasters billboard has been shaded in vertical strips to make it look as if it has been pieced together from multiple sheets. Only one tiny corner turned down gives any hint of destruction.

4 The corner is folded down by first masking the corner of the poster – a layer clipping path does the job without interfering with the layer mask. Now, on a new layer, draw the outline of the fold. Fill with a neutral color, and add a little shading with Dodge and Burn; then apply the Plastic Wrap filter to give the impression of sticky glue.

2 The first step is to create the tears. Make a layer mask for the poster layer, and make ragged selection using the Lasso tool. If you set the background color to black, you'll be able to remove chunks of poster simply by pressing *Delete*. Because we're working on a mask, we can always undo any deletions that seem inappropriate later.

3 Simply removing pieces of poster isn't enough. We need to show the torn paper around each rip. Make a new layer, grouped with the poster layer, and paint on it using a small, hard-edged brush to trace roughly around each tear. It's important not to try to be too precise here: the rougher the painting, the more convincing the effect.

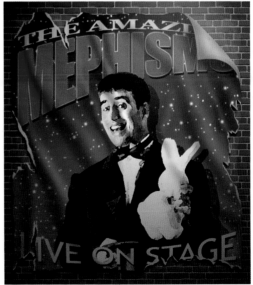

5 The folds and creases are added using Dodge and Burn, using the same technique outlined on the previous pages: first add a dark shadow using the Burn tool, then hold the ⌥ *alt* key (to temporarily access the Dodge tool) and paint above it to add the highlight. The lettering, which previously appeared flat, now looks rippled.

6 The lighting is added by making a new layer set to Hard Light mode, and filled with a neutral gray (it's an option when creating a Hard Light layer). Lighting Effects then adds both light and shade transparently through the layer. The drop shadow and the slight remains of old glue on the wall are both added as separate layers.

Waving the flag

1 PostScript flags, banners and crests of all kinds are widely available, both on the internet and as part of clip art collections. Photographs of real flags are harder to come by, especially as cutout objects; but it's relatively easy to make our own.

THE ILLUSTRATION ABOVE was commissioned by the Sunday Telegraph to accompany a story about the tribulations of Freeserve, the internet service provider. The holes in the flag were made by selecting ragged areas on a layer mask with the Lasso tool and filling with black; the rough strands at the edges of the holes were created by smudging with the Smudge tool on the mask itself.

Any flag, banner or flat artwork can be made to ripple convincingly in the breeze using the technique outlined here. I've started with a PostScript flag, but it's easy enough to apply any company logo instead.

4 The Shear filter is applied once again, this time horizontally. This makes the left edge of the flag look as if it's being held by the top and bottom on a flagpole; it also prevents the edge of the star panel from looking too rectilinear.

7 Now we can add the intricate creases and folds to the flag, following the Dodge and Burn technique described earlier in this chapter. Because we lowered the brightness in step 6, the Dodge tool still has its effect: if we hadn't done so, it would have made no difference to the white stripes.

2 As a first step, we'll apply some texture to the flag using the Texturizer filter. On the previous page we used the Canvas effect; here, though, we'll use the looser weave of Burlap instead, set to a small size and applied at a fairly low opacity.

3 The flag is rotated 90° and waved using the Shear filter (see earlier in this chapter), then rotated back again and distorted using Free Transform to make the right edge smaller than the left. This gives it more of a sense of perspective.

5 Because there's so much white in the flag, we need to reduce the overall brightness or our shading won't show up properly. Use the Curves or Levels dialogs to bring the highlights down slightly.

6 Basic shading is added in the same way as on our dollar bill, earlier in this chapter. This simply accentuates the gross waves of the flag, showing us which parts are rippling towards us and which are rippling away.

8 While the left edge of the flag looks convincing, the right edge appears too straight and uniform. This end isn't being held by anything, as the left was, and needs to flutter more. This is achieved simply by drawing a wavy path with the Pen tool, and hiding the edge with a layer mask.

9 When positioned on a pole and placed on a suitable background, the flag will still tend to look a little artificial. This is because flags are not solid objects: to blend it into the background, reduce the opacity of the layer slightly. Here, an opacity of 85% merges it in well.

HOT TIP

If you open an EPS illustration of a flag as a new Photoshop document, it will default to opening as a CMYK file. You may not notice anything wrong until you start to add texture, when you'll find that the Texturizer filter (along with several others) is dimmed out. Change the mode to RGB, or import it as an RGB file in the first place, to make these filters usable.

SHORTCUTS
MAC WIN BOTH

Ribbon and tape

1 Begin by drawing a path using the Pen tool. Keep the curves smooth, avoiding tight turns and corners. When you've finished, save the path and duplicate it before continuing – we'll need this half of it later.

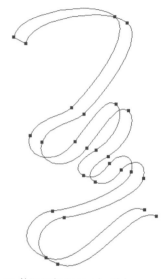

2 Now make a second path by selecting the original, and holding ⌥ *alt* as you offset it. Join the two starting points to make the two paths into one (holding ⌥ *alt* again, this time to force a corner at the join).

THE ILLUSTRATION ABOVE is part of a much larger montage for .net magazine about online stalkers. Dozens of photographs had to be fixed to the wall; shading on each one helped it look like it sat in place. The tape across the corner of some of the photos helped fix them to the wall in the reader's eye.

Ribbons can be used for a variety of purposes – from festooning partygoers to wrapping birthday presents. They're easier to draw than you might think; the trick is all in duplicating the Pen path.

1 We're going to fix this photograph to the wall using sticky tape. Begin by tracing the outline with the Lasso tool, holding ⌥ *alt* to draw the straight lines between the sides. Keep these sides parallel!

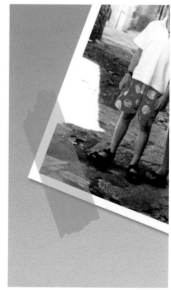

2 We don't need to make this tape solid, since it's made of translucent plastic. Let's fill the selected area with 50% gray. (It would also be possible to fill with solid gray, then reduce the layer opacity.)

3 Turn the path into a selection by pressing ⌘ *Enter* *ctrl* *Enter*. The ribbon will have some bumps where the paths crossed; these need filling by just painting across them. Dodge and Burn add some basic random shading.

4 We now need to add shading in the hollows. Activate the original path and turn it into a selection: nudge the selection down, and you'll find that the areas beneath the folds are selected ready for Dodge and Burn.

5 All that's needed now is a but of color. The Hue and Saturation dialog, set to Colorize, is one of the best ways to add dense color to a gray image.

3 Now add a little random shading, once again using Dodge and Burn. This is only a preliminary stage before we apply the Plastic Wrap filter. I've shown the tape isolated as well, for extra clarity.

4 The Plastic Wrap filter makes that shading look convincingly like reflective plastic. This useful filter is covered in more depth in Chapter 6, Shiny Surfaces.

5 Now color is added using Color Balance, which I find useful for subtle color effects; a lot of yellow and a little red does the trick. Brightness and contrast are increased slightly to make the tape shinier.

HOT TIP

When the ribbon path was offset in step 4 of the first workthrough, I didn't align it precisely with the right edge of the ribbon. By offsetting it by just a pixel or two, it was possible to use the shading to give the ribbon a slight thickness simply by leaving the edge unshaded.

SHORTCUTS

177

Upgrade and replace

THE FIRST COMPUTER I ever bought was a Sinclair Spectrum, which I purchased in 1980. It was a state-of-the-art machine, and I remember debating whether to choose the 16K version or opt for the massive 48K model. After much soul searching, I chose the 48K version: after all, I reasoned, this one was future-proof. Today, that computing power would barely run a singing greetings card.

The classified ads columns of newspapers and computer magazines are littered with advertisements from readers who have decided it's time to upgrade their equipment, and want to recoup the cost of their original purchase. Frequently, the prices demanded are well in excess of the aged computer's true value: often, readers will ask for more than it would cost to buy a new machine that offers twice as much power.

Their reasoning runs as follows: I bought this computer three years ago, and now it's obsolete thanks to the software developers, in league with the Devil and Bill Gates, who have upped the requirements for their new versions so much that they won't run on my old machine. And I'm damned if I'm going to shell out that much money simply to run Photoshop 7, so I want my money back before I commit myself to buying a new computer.

It's a fallacious argument, for several reasons. The first is that there's nothing wrong with their old computer. It will still run the software they used on it when they bought it, it will still access the internet at the same speed and it will still enable them to do their job in the same way as they have for the last three years. If they want to take advantage of the tempting features the latest software versions have to offer, then they'll need compatible hardware; otherwise, they can just stick with the software they already have.

You can't blame software for needing a higher specified operating platform each time it brings new functionality: if this wasn't the case, we'd still be editing images one black and white pixel at a time on our Spectrums. The demands made by Photoshop are colossal in terms of processing power, disk access and chip speed; only the most diehard Luddite would advocate the withdrawal of new features simply in order to ensure compatibility with antique equipment.

But the main problem I have with those who complain about the cost of upgrading is that they rarely take into account how much work their computer has done for them in the intervening period. My Mac enables me to do all my illustration work, as well as letting me do my accounts, watch DVDs and play Tomb Raider, for a relatively tiny cost compared with the revenue I generate from it. At the end of its three-year lifespan I reckon it now owes me nothing; the only hesitation I have in deciding when to upgrade is the knowledge that it will take a week for me to transfer all my applications and get the new machine running as smoothly as the old one. In return, I'll get a computer that's more than twice as fast, with a hard disk vast enough to hold the library of Alexandria.

Many computer users resent the fact that not just computers but memory and hard disks now cost just a fraction of what they paid for them several years earlier. They feel cheated in retrospect: if only they'd held on another couple of years they'd have been able to buy more power for less cost. What they ignore is the amount of work their equipment has done for them in the intervening period, which can usually be valued at far more than the few hundred extra they may have spent on it.

I now consider the ownership of my computer to be more like a rental than an outright purchase. I need to top up your payments every few years, in return for which I get a pristine new piece of technology that has none of the grouchiness my old computer acquired over the years, and offers blistering speed in return. And I even have the opportunity to pass my old machine on to an aged relative or impecunious acquaintance – or, failing that, to convert it into a state-of-the-art fishtank. And I only resent the cost of the new one for a week or two.

9 The third dimension

Talk to many Photoshop artists about 3D and they'll start screaming. That's because the intricacies of conventional 3D modeling programs are so unforgivingly awkward that the mysteries of Nurbs and B-splines are better suited to engineers than artists.

But who said anything about convention? There's a lot that can be achieved directly in Photoshop, without recourse to any other applications. Simulating 3D needn't be a nightmare.

There are times, however, when Photoshop alone just isn't enough. Dimensions, that cranky old application ignored by Adobe for so long, can be just the job for creating quick and dirty 3D models that provide the base for stunning Photoshop artwork.

Adding depth to flat artwork

ONE OF THE MOST COMMON TASKS the photomontage artist has to contend with is changing the viewpoint of an original photograph. Sometimes you can get away with simply rotating an object to make it fit in the scene; usually, it's a little more complicated.

The problem comes when an object has been photographed head-on, and you want to view it from an angle. Not all objects lend themselves to the kind of three-dimensional amendments shown here, but the principle used on these pages can be applied to a wide variety of source images.

1 This guitar has been photographed directly from the front, in common with many objects sourced from stock photography collections. In real life, you'd hardly ever see an object in this position: and placing it in a montage will always look flat and unconvincing.

2 The simplest way to change its perspective is to use Free Transform, holding ⌘ ⌥ Shift / ctrl alt Shift while dragging one of the corner handles to get a perspective distortion. The problem is immediately clear: there's no side to this guitar.

1 This old coin has been photographed directly from above; with close-up photography, an angled view would have made it difficult to keep the entire coin in focus. But we can create any view of this object we like with just a few actions.

2 The first step is to use Free Transform to squeeze the coin vertically: if you hold ⌥ / alt then it will squeeze towards its centre. You may wish to add perspective distortion as well, but it isn't really necessary.

3 Then select the coin by holding ⌘ / ctrl and clicking on its thumbnail in the Layers palette. Using the Move tool, hold ⌥ / alt as you nudge this selection up one pixel at a time using the Arrow keys, and you'll create this milled edge as you go.

HOW TO **cheat** IN
Photoshop

3 The side is best drawn with the Pen tool on a new layer, although you could also use the outline of the guitar as a starting point to get the curves correct. Here, the shape has simply been filled with a flat color to see if the perspective works.

4 A section of the guitar front is copied, duplicated and then flipped vertically to make a seamless tile. This is then used to fill the new side by grouping it with the side layer and repeating the pattern until it fills the space.

5 The key to realism lies, as ever, in the shading. The Burn tool has been set to Midtones to add the shadows – setting it to Highlights would have a more extreme effect, but would lose the warmth of the wood. Start slowly, and build up the shading.

4 That milled edge is perhaps a little too strong. To fix it, use `Shift` `⌘` `I` `Shift` `ctrl` `I` to invert the selection and make a new layer from the edge. Preserve transparency with `I` and fill with a color picked from the coin itself.

5 Now use the Dodge and Burn tools to add highlight and shadow to this new edge, using thin vertical strokes to create the illusion of light reflecting off the edge.

6 Since this was created on a new layer, we can simply lower its opacity to allow the 'original' milled edge to show through underneath.

HOT TIP

Boxy objects such as computer CPUs are easy to transform, even if photographed head-on. Simply copy a plain portion of the front of the unit, and distort it to form the side and top (if required). Adding appropriate shading means you can get away with a lot with little effort.

SHORTCUTS
MAC WIN BOTH

An open and shut case

ONE OF THE TRICKS THE PHOTOMONTAGE ARTIST needs to learn is how to make photographed objects do what he or she wants them to do – which means ignoring the perspective of the original image and adapting it to suit the needs of the job in hand.

The ability to open a closed door is a technique that every Photoshop professional should be able to achieve. Opening the drawer of the filing cabinet in our second example takes a keener eye, since it's important to match the rather distorted view present in the original photograph. But in Photoshop, if it looks right then it is right: you just have to trust your eye.

1 This door has been photographed closed, but opening it is simple. To begin, use the rectangular selection tool **M** to draw a rectangle that includes just the door itself, and not the frame. Cut this to a new layer using *Shift* ⌘ *J* *Shift* ctrl *J*.

1 The technique used to open the bottom drawer of this filing cabinet can equally well be applied to a wide range of tasks. Unlike the door, above, the drawer front doesn't hinge, so we can't use the perspective distortion in the same way.

2 Outline the drawer using the Pen tool, and make a it into new layer using ⌘ *J* ctrl *J*. It needs enlarging slightly, since it will be nearer to us; and a small amount of perspective distortion is required to match the extreme angle of the original.

3 Now reload the original selection by selecting the path and pressing *Enter* (the advantage of having created a Pen path) and make a new layer for the inside of the cabinet. Fill it with a dark gray, and add shading using the Burn tool to give the sense of depth.

2 Now use Free Transform ⌘ T / ctrl T to distort the door to its new position. If you hold ⌘ ⌥ Shift / ctrl alt Shift while dragging a corner handle you'll get a true perspective distortion; use the center handles to make the door narrower.

3 The thickness of the door is easy to make: draw a rectangular selection that includes part of the front edge of the door (but not the handle), make a new layer from it and flip it horizontally. Drag it into place, and then just darken it up.

4 The doorknob didn't take well to its perspective distortion, but it's easy to make an elliptical selection of the knob and distort it back to its correct shape. Since the door is a separate layer, darkening the interior on the layer below is child's play.

4 The drawer side is drawn on a new layer placed behind the drawer front by simply outlining it with the Lasso and filling with a mid gray. The three ribs are then drawn by selecting with the Lasso, and the areas between darkened with the Burn tool.

5 Once an object is placed in the drawer, the whole scene begins to make more sense. You need to choose objects to fill the cabinet that have a similar perspective to them; filling it with objects photographed head-on will look unconvincing.

6 The final stage is to add the shading – behind the folder in the drawer, and beneath the drawer itself. Make a new layer, grouped with the base cabinet layer, and paint on this using a soft-edged brush with black paint set to around 40%.

HOT TIP

When you use perspective distortion to open a door, you'll also need to reduce the width of the door to match: the more open it is (and the stronger the distortion), the narrower it will have to be. There's no solid rule for how to do this – just make sure it looks right.

SHORTCUTS
MAC WIN BOTH

185

Matching existing perspective

1 This shuttered shopfront is an ideal surface on which to place our sign. Not only does it have strong perspective lines, which will allow us to place the text accurately, it also includes a good bumpy texture that will make the finished result more convincing.

IN THIS ILLUSTRATION for the Sunday Telegraph, I aligned some of the elements with the perspective of the shutters. But the large Closed sign was placed at a deliberately skewed angle, to make it look as if it had been pasted on in a hurry. The sign still had to appear in perspective, but this was achieved purely by eye using Free Transform. (See Chapter 8 for details on shading the paper sign.)

In this workthrough, we'll look at how to make a shop sign that looks like it was photographed with the original shop.

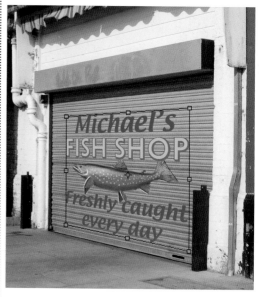

4 Select Free Transform (or press ⌘ T ctrl T). Hold ⌘ ctrl and grab a corner, then hold Shift as well after beginning to drag to constrain the movement to vertical. Align the top and bottom so that they line up with the ribs on the shutter.

2 The sign consists of four elements: the three sets of words, and the fish. Although it would have been possible to create all the text in a single block, you get far more control over size and spacing when they're kept as separate chunks of text.

3 Link all the sign elements together, and choose New Set From Linked in the pop-out menu on the Layers palette. Duplicate that set by dragging it onto the folder icon at the bottom (or choosing Duplicate from the pop-out menu), and then merge the new set so it becomes one layer.

5 The previous step got the sign into perspective, but it didn't look as if it was part of the image. Changing the layer mode to Multiply (use the menu at the top of the Layers palette) allows the original texture to show through, which looks far more convincing.

6 Placing the figure in front of the sign achieves two things: first, it adds a human element to the image; and second, by obscuring a tiny part of the sign it makes the sign look far more integrated into the final image.

HOT TIP

Not all surfaces have as obligingly clear perspective lines as this one. To work on an image without these indicators, it can help to place a simple grid over the surface first, and then use that to help align the text and other elements.

SHORTCUTS
MAC WIN BOTH

Building boxes

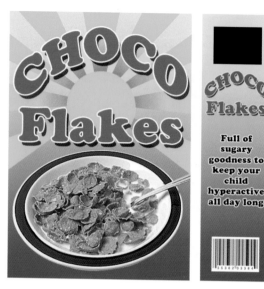

1 When preparing your flat artwork, remember that in most cases you'll be seeing the side of the box as well as the front, so you'll need to draw that as well. Keep a consistent color scheme on the side, and reuse some of the original artwork such as the Choco Flakes logo.

DRAWING BOXES IS EASY – it's simply a matter of distorting flat artwork using Free Transform, and adding a few finishing touches. The illustration above, for ES Magazine, was made slightly more complex by the fact that the box had a window in it, which meant drawing the polythene (see Chapter 6, Shiny Surfaces) and giving the inside of the lid a little thickness (using the techniques described earlier in this chapter). But the principles are exactly the same as with the breakfast cereal box used to demonstrate the process on these pages.

4 Darken the side of the box to make it stand out from the front. Then add some shading to the entire artwork using the Burn tool: a small amount of shadow helps it to look more like a real object and less like distorted flat artwork.

2 Create a merged copy so that you've got all the elements in one layer - that is, one for the front and one for the side. Then simply distort the front using Free Transform, holding ⌘ Shift ⌥ ctrl Shift alt and dragging a corner handle to make the perspective.

3 Now simply repeat the process for the side layer. If you only distorted the front of the box on the left-hand side, the side layer will still be the correct height and can be distorted in the opposite direction to make the box look three-dimensional.

5 Since this box is made of cardboard, you won't get a perfectly sharp edge where it bends around the corner. Here, I've selected a couple of pixels down the left-hand edge of the side and brightened that strip up to give the impression of the cardboard bending.

6 What makes an illustration like this work are the elements that break out of the planes, such as the spout on the right. And where would any self-respecting cereal be without a plastic toy? The wrap for this was created using Plastic Wrap - see Chapter 6 for how to do this.

HOT TIP

You can't keep text editable when applying perspective distortion – it needs to be rasterized first. So make sure you (and your client) are happy with the base artwork before turning it into a 3D object, or you'll have to repeat the process all over again after they've made the changes.

SHORTCUTS

MAC WIN BOTH

189

Wrapping labels round curves

1 This view of an oil drum presents a tricky problem for label wrapping. Firstly, it's a curved rather than a flat surface; and secondly, that surface has been photographed in perspective. So here's how it's done.

2 The label is created using suitable text and graphics. Although these were necessarily made on separate layers, it's important to merge them into one so that the distortions can be applied to everything together.

WRAPPING LABELS around curved surfaces can be a tricky proposition. In the illustration above for The Independent, I had to break the text into several chunks and distort each one using the Wave filter in order to make it look as if it was wrapped around the plastic surface.

5 Now rotate the canvas back again, and use Free Transform to apply a simple perspective distortion to the label. Don't expect it to look perfect; a close fit will be enough at this stage. To avoid fiddling around, it's easier to apply final tweaking to the misfit characters afterwards.

6 To make the lettering fit the perspective of the barrel, we need to select the troublesome letters (the beginnings and ends of each word) individually, and shear them vertically until they fit. A bitty font like Stencil is easiest to work with, as you can distort letter sections in chunks.

3 The first distortion is to Spherize the label, so it looks more as if it's wrapped around a cylinder. In the Spherize dialog, use Horizontal Only rather than the full Spherize, so that it's only distorted in the horizontal dimension.

4 Now to bend the label using the Shear filter. This filter will only distort horizontally, so we must first rotate the canvas 90°. The filter works by drawing points on the straight line, which can be dragged out into curves; the preview shows the distortion.

7 To retain the texture of the original, load up the area of the distorted label (⌘ ctrl click on the name in the Layers palette), hide it, switch to the base layer and float the selection using ⌘ J ctrl J. Now simply use Hue/Saturation to colorize the label.

8 The label still looks a little unconvincing, so to strengthen it up change the Layer mode from Normal to Multiply – this will accentuate the shadows, making the finished label look far more like it's sitting on the object in the real world.

HOT TIP

If you're working on a large document, rotating the whole thing 90° to apply the Shear filter will take an age. Instead, you can simply copy the base object to a new document, rotate that, and then copy the resulting distortion back into your original image.

SHORTCUTS
MAC WIN BOTH

191

Editable text on 3D surfaces

1 The basic label text (below) has been distorted using the Warp Text feature. The Arch setting has been given a Bend value of -57 (see screen shot at bottom), so it curves downwards. As it stands, the text doesn't fit the label; the next step will bring the fit closer.

THE WARP TEXT FEATURE introduced in Photoshop 6 is seen by many as a flashy special effect with little practical application. But it's a useful tool for fitting text onto curved three-dimensional surfaces, as we'll see in this example using a medicine bottle as the base object.

Because the Warp Text effect works with live text, we can go back and edit the text at any point - changing the wording, color, font or type size as we wish, without having to go through any of the steps outlined in the previous pages.

I discovered this technique while working on the job above, in which the client couldn't be certain about the precise wording needed, but wanted to see how the effect would look before continuing. The ability to change just the text at the last minute made it possible to complete the job on time.

DRUGS-R-US

Aspirin

To be taken as directed – follow
the instructions on reverse.

2 Now, simply shearing the text box vertically using Free Distort enables us to pull the left side of the text down so that it more closely approximates the label. Grab a center handle to add the shear effect. Because it's not a perspective or free distortion, we can perform it while the text remains editable: simple shearing is one of the distortions (along with scaling and rotation) that's 'allowed' on live text.

3 Because the bottle has been viewed from above, with a strong perspective, the label appears narrower at the bottom than at the top. To fix this, we can use the two additional distortion sliders.

A negative value for the Vertical Distortion (see below) makes the text taper inwards at the bottom; and a tiny negative value for the Horizontal Distortion makes it slightly wider at the left than at the right.

In practice, you'll find yourself tweaking all the sliders several times until the correct curve is found; but most surfaces can be conformed to with this technique.

4 Because the text remains editable throughout, we can go back at any point and alter what it says. As long as the longest line remains the same width, the distortion will remain the same; if it's short, add spaces to fit.

5 To make the text more convincing, duplicate the layer, rasterize the text and blur it. Since we've kept the original unrasterized version, we can still edit that if necessary.

HOT TIP

Not all surfaces can be matched as easily as this one. There are two tricks for dealing with more complex geometries: either type spaces after the longest line to force an asymmetric distortion, or break the text into two halves and distort each one individually.

Warp Text

Style: Arch

◉ Horizontal ○ Vertical

OK

Cancel

Bend: -57 %

Horizontal Distortion: -1 %

Vertical Distortion: -5 %

SHORTCUTS
MAC WIN BOTH

Drawing pipes and cables

1 Drawing cables and wires is easier than you might think. Start by using the Pen tool to draw a Bézier curve that follows the line you wish the cable to take.

4 By nudging vertically and inversing the selection, only the feathered bottom half of the cable is selected. We can now use Brightness and Contrast to darken the edge.

1 Begin your pipe by drawing a simple rectangle with the Marquee tool, and filling it with a mid-tone gray (you can always add color later).

4 With the ⌥ *alt* key still held down, drag the ellipse to the other end: hold the *Shift* key after dragging to move it horizontally only.

6 With the Marquee tool selected, nudge the selection a couple of pixels to the right and fill with the same mid gray. The bright rim looks better than a hard edge.

8 Draw a new selection with the Elliptical Marquee that's smaller than the original one, and add shading to make the inside of the pipe – darker at the top and on the left.

WHETHER IT'S MICROPHONE CABLES, sewage pipes or chrome cylinders, it's fairly easy to create any kind of tubular object directly in Photoshop.

Cables are drawn using the technique of applying a brush stroke to a Pen-drawn path: as long as the path is visible, any of the painting tools can be easily made to run a smooth stroke along it.

Pipes can be created at any length. Since the shading is applied evenly along the pipe by holding the Shift key as you paint with the Dodge and Burn tools, it's then easy to stretch them to any length you want simply by selecting half the pipe and dragging a copy where you want it to go.

Bending pipes around curves is another issue entirely, and the final step here shows a simple way to achieve this effect.

2 Now, with the Pen path still selected, switch to the Brush tool and choose a hard-edged brush of the right diameter – here, a 9-pixel brush was used. Now hit the `Return` key, and the path will be stroked with that brush.

3 Next, load up the pixels in the cable layer by holding `⌘` `ctrl` as you click on the layer's name. Feather the selection (a 3-pixel feather used here), and, with the Marquee tool selected, nudge the selection up 3 pixels.

5 Now nudge the selection down twice as many pixels as you nudged it up (that makes 6, in this instance) and brighten up the top half in the same way.

6 After coloring the cable, it's time for the shadow. Modify your original path so that parts of the cable rise up from the floor, then stroke the path with a soft-edged brush.

2 Using the Dodge and Burn tools set to Highlights, hold the `Shift` key to constrain the motion to horizontal, as you drag from end to end of the rectangle.

3 Now use the Elliptical Marquee tool to select an ellipse in the center of the pipe. Hold `⌥` `alt` to make a copy as you drag it to the left to form the end of the pipe.

HOT TIP

When using shading techniques such as those shown here, it's always better to work with gray objects rather than colored ones: shading can affect the color as well as the luminance of an image. When the shading is exactly how you want it, you can put the color in using Color Balance, Curves or your favorite tool.

5 Now brighten up the selected end of the pipe, using Brightness and Contrast or Curves. It's brighter than we need, but this will just form the rim around the edge.

Polar Coordinates

OK

Cancel

33%

Options:
⦿ Rectangular to Polar
◯ Polar to Rectangular

7 With the end cap still selected, add some more shading using the Burn tool. Bear the lighting position in mind: we want more shadow at the bottom right than at the top.

10 To bend the pipe into a curve, make a square selection around it and use the Polar Coordinates filter (Rectangular to Polar) to distort it. If the pipe is positioned at the top of the square selection, the result will be a very tight curve; if it's positioned in the center, you'll get a larger curve. Make sure the initial selection is square or the curve will be distorted. You can now take a section of this curved pipe to join two straight pieces together.

9 By applying a step effect using the Curves dialog, we can make this pipe look more metallic. See Chapter 7 for details on how to achieve this effect.

SHORTCUTS
MAC WIN BOTH

3D modeling applications

W HILE YOU CAN DRAW just about anything you can imagine directly in Photoshop – if you have the time and the skill – there are times when a basic 3D modeling application can help you out of a tight spot. First of all, let me lay my cards on the table: I hate 3D modelers. I loathe the intricacies of Nurbs and B-splines, and resent the time taken sitting around waiting for models to render.

That's why I like Dimensions, the elderly 3D program produced by Adobe. It can perform just two basic functions: extruding (adding depth) and revolving (lathing a profile). But where it really scores is that it's the only 3D program to

export PostScript artwork – in the form of Illustrator objects. This means they're infinitely scalable, and so can be enlarged to any size you like. Rendering time is just a few seconds; after that, you can take the model into Photoshop and enhance it.

Dimensions hasn't been updated since 1997, and suffers a number of drawbacks: it's clumsy, buggy, and none of the keyboard shortcuts work with recent operating system releases. That said, it still performs its task admirably – and you can always use a macro program, such as QuicKeys, to replace the keyboard shortcuts for you.

The trick with Dimensions is not to expect too much from it. While it is capable of rendering shading from multiple light sources, because it exports PostScript artwork the shading is create as stepped blends; some blurring is often needed afterwards in Photoshop to fix this.

Dimensions illustrations occasionally go wrong: bits will be missing when the illustration is rendered, for instance. There's no support for transparency, and the texturing is so laughable as to be completely unusable.

One quick alternative is 3D Invigorator from Zaxwerks (www.zaxwerks.com), a Photoshop plug-in that can extrude Illustrator outlines and render them as beautiful 3D images within Photoshop. With complex bevels, shiny surfaces and powerful lighting tools, Invigorator should be the ideal solution – except that you can't generate the outlines within the software; they have to be imported from Illustrator. For quick 3D, it's a nice plug-in.

Then there's Amorphium (www.play.com), the bizarre modeler that creates organic images – and renders them at enormous size in seconds. Fun to use, it can be hard to make it do what you want; but what you end up with is usually worth the struggle.

For the Photoshop user who simply wants to get a quick model to work on, Dimensions – despite its many shortcomings – remains the best choice. Over the next few pages we'll look at some of the artwork created using Dimensions models as their base. Even if you're only exporting a basic outline model, creating such objects as a perspective box can be done in seconds in Dimensions: the same illustration

might take hours to create in Photoshop.

The illustrations I'll discuss in the rest of this chapter all use Dimensions as their starting point, but I'll stress that the program can't generate anything near finished artwork. I won't go through a step by step tutorial showing how to create the models in Dimensions itself; instead I'll discuss how to make these simple PostScript models come to life, using the tools and techniques in Photoshop. If you want to try Dimensions for yourself, you'll find a demo copy on the CD that accompanies this book.

ABOVE: *Amorphium is a 3D modeling tool that's by turns fun, exhilarating and infuriating. But if you want organic forms, it's a good choice and is easy enough to learn.*

LEFT: *3D Invigorator is a Photoshop plug-in that can extrude and perspectivize Illustrator outlines. The results are impressive – but the tools can be hard to manage.*

197

Remote, but in control

1 This was a simple model to create in Dimensions: a curved bevel was added to the remote's outline to give the rounded effect. The model was then saved in two parts: first the buttons were hidden, the model rendered as a PostScript image and then saved as an EPS file; then the buttons were revealed and the base hidden, and exported as a separate image.

THIS IMAGE was created for the Radio Times magazine to accompany a story about two new BBC television channels. The remote control's buttons had to be oversized to get the point across: the four BBC buttons were to be made the most prominent, with buttons for the other channels hidden behind the hand holding it.

While photographing an existing remote control might have seemed the obvious choice, the task of getting rid of the original buttons made this an impractical route. Adobe Dimensions was the obvious choice to construct the basic model, providing a good starting point with which to work.

5 I keep a selection of hands (many of them my own) to use for holding a variety of objects. This one fitted the remote perfectly, and a layer mask was used to tuck the bottom of the remote behind the base of the thumb. This is exactly the same technique as that outlined in Chapter 2, Hiding and Showing.

2 This is the basic model imported into Photoshop in two layers. By creating the model in two parts we've managed to keep the elements separate, so that they can be treated individually.

3 The buttons were given a degree of shininess by brushing over them with the Dodge and Burn tools. An area was then defined within the remote and a new layer created; this was then filled with a dark gray, followed by Gaussian Noise and then Gaussian Blur to soften the effect. The slight blue tint was simply added using Color Balance.

4 The Noise/Blur layer was selected and its perimeter expanded by 3 pixels; on a new layer, this rim was shaded using Dodge and Burn to create an inner bevel. The red plastic cover at the top of the remote was created by making a new layer from an elliptical selection that intersected the base. This was then filled with a dark red, and the leading edge was brightened up.

HOT TIP

Since this image was destined for the printed page, it was important to ensure it would work in CMYK. This was particularly relevant when adding highlights to the colored buttons, since these are areas where an image can easily go out of gamut. After highlighting each one, I used Hue and Saturation to colorize it: by flipping in and out of CMYK Preview mode (⌘ Y ctrl Y) I could check when the button was too bright, and reduce the saturation accordingly.

6 Because the hand was simply dumped on top of the remote, it looked artificial and unconvincing. The bottom edge of the hand was shaded using the Burn tool; then a new layer was created beneath it, onto which a soft shadow was painted using the Brush tool set to 50% opacity - this allowed me to build up the shadow gradually where needed.

7 The glow effect within the lit-up buttons was added using the Dodge tool to highlight them; the edges, previously very dark, were brightened considerably. The buttons were then each colorized using the Hue/Saturation dialog. The seating for the buttons was added by creating a Pillow Emboss using Layer Effects, which made the bed of the remote look like it was cut to receive the buttons.

8 The text and symbols were typed and drawn as appropriate, and skewed into the correct perspective to fit the buttons. Placed below the shadow layer, they allowed the shading to appear on top of them. In order to give the impression of the text being incised into the buttons, the Emboss feature in Layer Effects was used again – this time, the usual direction was reversed to give the impression of depressed rather than raised buttons.

SHORTCUTS
MAC WIN BOTH

A piece of cake

1 The model was created in just a few minutes in Dimensions. A rolling bevel was used to give a slight undulation to the edge of the cake. In the end result, almost nothing remained of the original model - but it served its purpose as a useful template to build the illustration around.

OFTEN, THE MOST BASIC 3D MODEL can be used as the starting point for a realistic illustration. In this instance, the brief was to draw a cake in the shape of the Channel 4 logo for a story about a proposed sell-off (carving up the cake — when in doubt, pounce on a ready-made metaphor). While it would have been possible to create this illustration entirely in Photoshop, using the Free Transform tool to create the perspective, the ability to generate a simple 3D model makes it easier to get started.

This illustration uses a combination of drawn elements (the cake and the icing) and real photographs - notably the cake texture. While it would be possible to draw this texture, it would be hard to do convincingly; and after all, that's what digital cameras are for.

5 The cake was then merged into a single layer, and the tip cut off in a jagged line using the Lasso tool. This was made into a new layer to allow the two elements to be handled independently. The crumbs around the cake were made by drawing small selections over the original texture in QuickMask, then moving them down to their new position. The rectangles making up the logo were also strengthened to make them easier to read.

2 I started by creating a selection using the top and wavy edge of the cake to make a new layer, which was then colored pink, to which a small amount of Gaussian Noise was added. Noise prevents forms drawn in Photoshop from appearing too shiny, which would detract from their plausibility as real-world objects.

3 A scan of a piece of real cake was placed beneath the icing layer, and grouped with the base model so that it only showed where it overlapped the model. The icing layer now looked too pasty by comparison, so its strength was increased simply using Brightness and Contrast.

4 Plastic Wrap was used in moderation to add a shine to the surface of the cake, giving it an additional gloss. The cream was painted on a new layer using a soft-edged brush; this was then filled with a small amount of Gaussian Noise, and shaded using the Dodge and Burn tools set to Midtones.

HOT TIP

There are times when too many layers just get in the way - such as when we want to cut a slice off, as in step 5. Rather than merging the layers irrevocably, it's better to create a Layer Set using all the elements so far, duplicate that set and merge the duplicate to create a single layer. An easy alternative is to hide all but the layers you want to merge, make a new layer, then use

⌘ ⌥ Shift E
ctrl alt Shift E

to make a merged copy of all the visible elements in the new layer.

6 Cake texture and cream were copied from elsewhere in the cake and placed behind the cutoff section, following the perspective made by the slicing. A silver cake slice placed behind this gave it a reason to be floating in mid-air.

7 The background was a solid fill of 50% Cyan, 25% Yellow: on top of this, a Black to Transparent Gradient Adjustment Layer was placed to create the shading. By keeping this shading on a separate layer, it was possible to adjust it later for both position and opacity.

8 These seemingly complex reflections were surprisingly easy to create. The cake was duplicated, and a Wave filter applied: this was then dragged to the back of the artwork, and the opacity reduced accordingly. The reflections of the crumbs, cake slice and sliced cake were created in the same way.

Dimensions: bits and pieces

1 This exploded Union Jack was for a story in The Guardian about suggested redesigns for the national flag. Once I'd conceived the idea for the illustration, Dimensions was the natural choice: I simply imported a Union Jack and twisted each section individually. In this case, rather than rendering a finished model I copied the PostScript outlines and pasted them directly into Photoshop as paths: that way, I could isolate each section and color and shade it separately from the rest.

MODELS BUILT IN DIMENSIONS don't always need to form the bulk of the illustration. Often, there's just one element that is either difficult or impossible to photograph, yet is easy to create as a 3D model. The advantage of making simple models is that, unlike photographed objects, there's no fiddly cutting out to be done; in the case of the wireframe globe on the facing page, even if there had been a suitable photograph, tracing

around each strut of the wire would have been an endless task.

The images on this page were all commissioned jobs which would have been tricky to create without a 3D modeler on hand. Since newspaper work is always completed to tight deadlines – often just a couple of hours – the speed of Dimensions in rendering even large images makes it a better solution than waiting for a high-end modeler to finish.

2 This illustration was for a Guardian feature about dumbing down – specifically, the horrors of globalization. The wireframe model was created as a series of semicircular hoops: the entire model was then rotated 180° about its axis to generate the wireframe in two sections. To get the metallic effect, I used the excellent Chrome filter in the EyeCandy 4000 filter suite (see Chapter 11).

The countries were drawn by wrapping a drawing of a globe around a sphere model, also in Dimensions, and then coloring and shading the result accordingly.

By creating the wireframe in two halves, I was able to place one at the back and one at the front, making it easy to arrange all the objects between the two. This trick of splitting a model in half is a useful one for a large variety of purposes: drawing a bottle or jar, for instance, in two halves makes it easy to place other objects inside them without having to worry about complicated masking procedures. Splitting things in half is also a useful technique for items like shopping baskets, waste paper bins and other see-through objects.

3 Modeling this sun bed (for an illustration for .net magazine) was simply a matter of placing a series of bevelled tubes next to each other: those ugly overlaps seen along the side in the original model were easy to smooth out in Photoshop. The shading wasn't as complex as it looks: it's the reflection of the man's arm and legs that makes the surface look like polythene.

The Poser phenomenon

*This image for
MacUser magazine
was to illustrate a
feature I wrote on
Poser. Models need a
fair amount of work
after you import
them into
Photoshop, cleaning
up jagged edges
around knees and
elbows, and
smoothing out odd
wrinkles in the skin;
but it makes a good
starting point for
cases where you
can't find the right
pose elsewhere.*

POSER IS A UNIQUE 3D MODELING
application. It has just one purpose: to
produce images of people, as realistically as
possible.

The realism of the application's output
increases with each new release, and it's getting
to the stage where the figures generated look
almost real. Almost, but not quite: you can still
tell that a figure has been generated rather
than photographed. Nevertheless, with a bit of
work in Photoshop it's possible to get

acceptable results from Poser without having to
go to the expense and inconvenience of hiring
models (or the embarrassment of asking them
to take their clothes off).

With its quirky interface (loosely copied by
Amorphium, as can be seen earlier in this
chapter) Poser looks and feels like no other
program. As well as being a powerful modeler,
it's also fun to use, as long as you've got
enough RAM: the latest version requires at least
200Mb assigned to it, and is far happier

Poser's interface may be off-putting to new users, but it's easy to use once you get the hang of manipulating your figures using the modeling tools. Rendering the final image only takes a few minutes, resulting in a TIFF file with an alpha channel that can be used to isolate the figure from its background. The dotted patches above and around the eyes indicate semi-transparent areas that are turned into eyebrows and eyelashes when the final render is performed.

operating with a whole lot more. Now published by its original developers, Curious Labs (www.curiouslabs.com), Poser comes with a range of reasonably convincing figures of its own; but if you want greater realism, you'll need to purchase additional models from Daz3D (www.daz3d.com) who, under the name Zygote, developed the original Poser models.

For the digital artist interested in generating photorealistic images, Poser is useful in that it's quick and easy to model any pose you like; using the Daz3D models, you can even change the physiognomy of the faces and bodies of your models to suit your needs.

Poser is also frustrating in that the figures never quite look real enough to fool even the most casual of readers: while the faces are getting better and better, clothing still tends to look like plastic. But Poser is great for generating crowds of out-of-focus figures to populate your backgrounds, for creating quick roughs or for building wireframe models for cases where you want a computer-generated look. I used Poser to build the head of the man on the front of this book, as we'll see in the next chapter.

A wide range of clothing, hair and tools is available, both from Daz3D and from many third party and shareware sources – one of the best is www.renderosity.com, who distribute a wide range of free and low-cost clothing, props and models from their website.

Reality overload

REALITY IS ALL VERY WELL, but it can be a little dull. Photoshop gives us the opportunity to make real life more exciting, more vivid and more dynamic. Throughout this book I've concentrated on techniques for making images look as realistic as possible; but we shouldn't let our desire for realism get in the way of a good picture.

We instinctively know when something looks plausible, and when it doesn't. We've all seen old films showing flying cars, rockets and men falling out of airplanes, and have sensed that the real thing wouldn't look that way. But how do we know what the real thing would look like? Most of us have never seen a rocket from space, or someone falling from a plane. It's likely that the 'real thing', when filmed, wouldn't look convincing either: in many cases, creating a plausible image is more important than one that adheres rigidly to the confines of reality.

Often, the way we remember an object or scene is of more importance than the prosaic reality. Let's say you wanted to draw a time bomb, to be incorporated in a montage. You could spend hours researching bomb construction on the Internet, and end up with a dull, colorless device that readers would find hard to interpret. Or you could simply draw two orange sticks attached by curly wires to an analog alarm clock, and you'd have an instantly recognizable image.

Let's take a different example. You're creating a montage of the President of the United States at his desk in the Oval Office. Without suitable reference material, you must rely on your memory – and the collective memory of your readers – to make the picture work. So you assemble a large desk, a high-backed chair, and a window with flags hanging either side of it. But what of the view through the window? It's likely that, should the President turn in his swivel chair, he'll gaze out over a dull stretch of White House lawn. For the reader, though, such a scene wouldn't help to place the location. If you instead opt for a view of another government building, perhaps with a glimpse of a dark-suited man in black sunglasses with a curly wire over his ear, you'll give the reader many more clues to where your scene is located.

Cartoons, both in print and in animation, have educated us to recognize a host of artificial visual devices designed to accentuate the action. So we'll always see a puff of smoke as Road Runner suddenly takes off for the hills; and we're so used to seeing characters carry on running in mid-air as they leave a cliff top (before suddenly plunging to their doom when they realize their predicament) that we don't think twice about the logic. In printed cartoons, we've come to interpret a series of wavy lines behind a running figure as indicating speed, and straight lines emanating from a central point as a sign of explosive activity.

These metaphors have become so much part of the public consciousness that we can adapt them for use in photomontage. The result will tend towards illustration, and few readers would be fooled into thinking these were actual photographs: but, sensitively used, the cartoonist's techniques can add life to an otherwise static composition.

In real life, explosions are scenes of chaos and confusion, usually so wreathed in smoke that you can't see what's going on. In Photoshop, we can start with the elements of the destruction and add fire, smoke and sparks to illuminate the scene; we're not so concerned with recreating the effect of a real explosion as we are with communicating to the reader that an explosion is taking place. Which means dipping into the collective subconscious to retrieve the sense of exploding material we've gathered from action movies.

If what you want to do is fool your public into thinking they're looking at a real photograph, then none of these techniques will apply. But if your aim is to create an illustration that's entertaining and that tells a story, then don't let the constraints of reality get in the way.

In the next chapter we'll look at a few ways of making reality just that little bit more exciting.

10 Hyper realism

FOR TIMES WHEN REALITY becomes too much to bear, we need to add illustrative elements that make a static picture look more dynamic. These move an image towards hyper realism: what we're depicting is no longer gritty realism, but a graphic illustration.

Real blurred photographs may give the sense of speed, but it's at the expense of clarity. By creating blurs and showing them selectively, we can give the impression of a fast-moving object without losing the detail. In this chapter we'll also look at how to make explosions and other scenes of destruction, as well as how to make complex scenes comprehensible.

Finally, we'll look at how many of the techniques outlined in this book have been combined to make the cover image.

Blurring for speed

1 Here's the proud owner of a new photomontage shop, photographed outside his premises. He's been positioned so we can see the sign behind him, but it's all rather lacking in dynamism; the empty space to the left of him badly needs filling.

THE ILLUSTRATION ABOVE was to illustrate a Sunday Telegraph article on the proposed merger of American Airlines and British Airways. It was a simple enough job: fitting the heads of the two airline bosses to the bodies, and placing the logos on the backs of seats. But I felt that as it stood, the image was too static: so I added a Radial Blur to give the impression of speed.

In this section we'll look at how to use blur techniques to give the impression of movement, and how to get the best results from the filters.

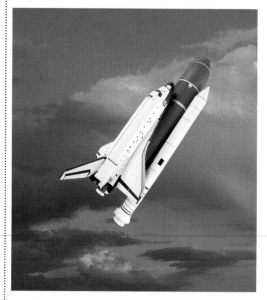

4 Here's a model of a space shuttle taking off into the skies. It's clearly not the real thing, and looks little better than a child's toy suspended against an unconvincing sky. Motion Blur, once again, can help bring this static image to life.

IMAGES: BODYSHOTS (PEOPLE), HEMERA PHOTO OBJECTS (SPACE SHUTTLE), COREL (SKY)

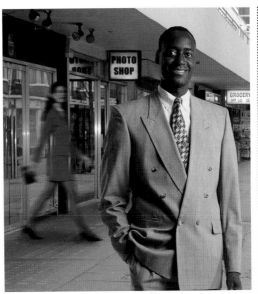

2 Placing a passer-by in the scene helps with the composition of the montage, and her bright red suit adds a much-needed splash of color. The trouble here is that she's too strong an element: she draws the eye away from the main focus of the picture.

3 Applying a small degree of Motion Blur to the figure makes it appear as if she happened to be walking past while the photograph was being taken, and knocks her more firmly into the background. Of course, in reality a person wouldn't be blurred as evenly as this; but the effect works.

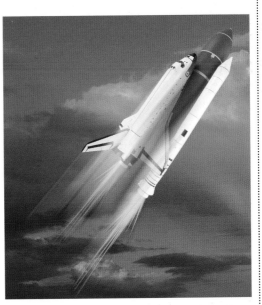

5 The shuttle layer is duplicated – we don't want to lose its sharp outline, only to add a blur on top. This layer is then blurred using Motion Blur. But the filter works in both directions: to make the shuttle look as if it's speeding forwards, we need to move either it or the blur.

6 By moving the shuttle to the top end of the blurred layer, the whole of the blur takes place behind it. The flames shooting out of the rocket boosters help: these are simply fireworks, merged in using the techniques described in Chapter 2, Hiding and Showing.

HOT TIP

The Motion Blur filter offers no preview within its dialog – instead, the blur is displayed on the whole image every time you make an adjustment. Getting the angle of the blur right can be tricky: but rather than dragging the direction wheel, highlight the Angle field and use the Up and Down cursor keys to change the angle of blur in small increments.

HOW TO **cheat** IN **Photoshop**

More blurring techniques

1 Here's our driverless sports car, careering out of control on a shopping street. The immediate problems are apparent: firstly, the car clearly isn't moving; and secondly, the angle of view of the car bears little relation to the street on which it's been placed.

BLURRING GIVES THE IMPRESSION of speed, but can also help to focus the reader's attention. The illustration above was for Men's Health, to show how wearing a hands-free headset would help to lower stress levels while driving (this was before it was suggested that hands-free headsets might fry your brains while you're chilling out). The car we want the reader to look at is buried amongst the traffic, but by blurring the vehicles around it I could ensure that the reader wouldn't be distracted by them.

On these pages I'll discuss how to make both Motion Blur and Radial Blur work together, to give the impression that a static car is really moving.

4 The first way to give an impression of movement is to add Radial Blur to the wheels. A circular selection is made into a new layer, which has Radial Blur (Spin) applied, as seen on the left; this is then masked (right) so that the car body is no longer blurred.

7 Motion Blur, as I explained on the previous page, works in both directions. But we only want the blur to show behind the car – not at the front, where it hasn't been yet. So the whole blurred layer is simply moved to the right so that it trails behind the vehicle.

2 Cars are complex shapes, and distorting its perspective would have been a laborious and probably impossible task. But it's easy to change the perspective of the street to match the car: Free Transform is all that is required. The shadow beneath the car also helps to position it.

3 Although the car has been cut out, the original backdrop was still visible through the window. Making a layer mask, we can hide the view through the window so the street is visible. Then, by reducing the contrast of the mask, we can make it appear as if we're looking through glass.

5 The whole car is then duplicated, and Motion Blur applied to the new layer. It's fairly easy to adjust the angle of the blur to match the dominant angle of the car, as the filter gives you a full-screen preview of its effect.

6 Because the car is viewed in perspective, the straight lines of the blur no longer match all the angles of the car. Using Free Transform, we can distort the blur to make it follow the perspective of the car reasonably well.

8 The blur hid too much of the original car, and blurred elements such as the wheels didn't look convincing. So we can simply make a layer mask for the blurred layer, and paint out those areas we want to hide: now we retain much of the car's detail, while keeping the sense of movement.

9 The whole image still looked too static: the car was clearly moving, but the sense of speed didn't come through. The answer is to add a little Motion Blur to the background as well, as if the photographer had tried to follow the car's motion but didn't quite manage it.

HOT TIP

Simply adding Motion Blur to a layer can have the effect of muddying the image, rather than adding a sense of speed to it. Blurred images will often need brightening up to make them work more convincingly; it's also worth experimenting with setting their layer modes to Screen or Hard Light to enhance the effect.

213

Breaking glass

1 The original screen on this television has been replaced by a new layer, tinted blue and accented using the Dodge tool to make it more appealing. Since the days of black and white TV, we're used to screens looking bluish.

BREAKING GLASS IN PHOTOSHOP has little to do with broken glass in real life, which tends to look dull and lifeless. We want to give the impression of serious damage, as in the illustration above for The Independent: the violence of the act must be more apparent than the actuality.

Here, we'll look at the process of smashing the glass on the front of a television screen: the glass will explode outwards to heighten the effect. In real life, of course, smashing a screen would cause the glass to implode inwards, to fill the vacuum inside the tube; but real life is sometimes too dull to reproduce.

On the following pages, we'll look at how to turn this broken screen into an explosion.

4 In the last step, we reduced the selection area to the original Lasso selection minus a thin border at the right edge. When we now exit QuickMask and delete, we're left with just the brightened edge of the glass to give some thickness to the broken edge.

7 Nudge the selection down a couple of pixels (don't use the Move tool or you'll move the layer), and use the Brush tool set to Behind to add some thickness to the glass. There will be some awkward double spikes at the pointed ends; these can be removed using the Eraser.

2 Using the Lasso tool, select an irregular shape on the screen and brighten it up. If you hold ⌥ *alt* while clicking points on the screen you can draw straight selection lines between the points.

3 Enter QuickMask mode by pressing **Q** and select the red mask with the Magic Wand. Nudge the selection up and left a couple of pixels; then inverse the selection and delete, so only a fraction of the highlight remains.

5 On a new layer, draw individual shards of glass with the Lasso tool – simple triangles work best. Using a soft brush at around 50% opacity, paint some color from the screen into these shards, but don't fill them completely.

6 Don't deselect, but use the Dodge tool to brighten up those shards so that they look more reflective. Again, use the tool unevenly so that the pieces don't end up looking too uniform in appearance.

8 Duplicate the glass shards layer, and use Free Transform to shrink the new layer towards the centre of the screen (hold the ⌥ *alt* key as you drag a corner handle). Lower the opacity of this new layer to around 50% to give the impression of movement.

9 Make another duplicate of this layer, and reduce that in size even further – you can add a small degree of rotation as well if you wish. Reduce the opacity of this layer still further, to around 20%, to complete the explosive effect. Finally, paint a little smoke inside the screen.

Smashing things up (1)

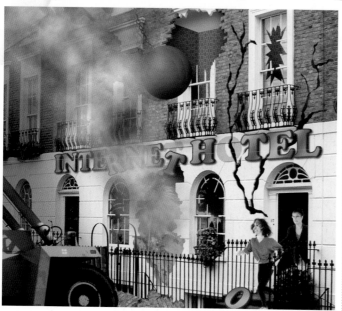

WHICH OF US HASN'T WANTED, at some time or other, to take a sledgehammer to our computer when it freezes? Or to our television during an election broadcast? With Photoshop, it's easy to vent your anger without voiding your insurance.

The illustration above was for a Sunday Telegraph article about the end of so-called Internet hotels. The fires and explosions simply add to the sense of chaos.

The principles of breaking up technology apply equally well to televisions as to hotels: it's a matter of making holes and then filling the gaps. Following on from the previous page, we'll look here at how to make a television explode.

1 Here's the same television we used before, placed against a black background. If you're going to use explosions and flying glass, the effect always works best against a dark background; explosions rarely show up well against white.

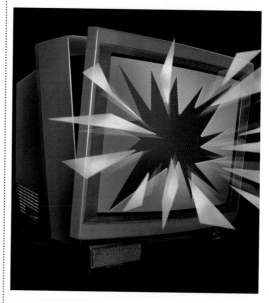

4 Now we can bring in the flying glass and broken screen from the previous page, rotating it to fit the new angle of the screen border. That's the basics of the television finished: all we need to do now is to add the elements that will make the destruction look more explosive.

2 Begin by selecting the front panel, then cut it to a new layer using *Shift* ⌘ *J* *Shift* *ctrl* *J*. It's now easy to distort it to a new position: although I've kept it close to the original, there's no reason why you shouldn't have it flying halfway across the room.

3 Repeat this process with the side, rotating it in the opposite direction. Add some shading with the Burn tool to give the effect of a shadow. You'll also need to draw the inside of the frame, on a new layer: simply fill the outline with a color picked from the TV, and shade it.

5 Fireworks make great explosions. This firework has been placed just in front of the rotated side, and the black background knocked out of it using the techniques described in Chapter 2. The back edge of the side was painted out on a layer mask so that the firework spilled out behind it.

6 The firework layer is duplicated to make a second explosion, and a bunch of other electronic material is added to give the impression of the guts of the TV flying out in disarray. Next time you upgrade your computer, remember to photograph the boards before throwing them away.

SHORTCUTS

Smashing things up (2)

ON THE PREVIOUS spread we looked at an explosion in the act of occurring, complete with sparks and flying glass. Here, we'll step forward in time to view the destruction after it's happened.

This piece of artwork for the Sunday Telegraph was for a story about the break-up of the telecommunications company Energis, graphically illustrated by a smashed telephone. It's a fiddly job, as each of the buttons on the handset needs to be isolated and distorted individually; but it simply takes a little patience to ensure that all the pieces fit where they belong.

Never having studied the interior of a telephone, I have no idea if they contain printed circuit boards or this sort of wiring. But this is artwork, not technical illustration; such niceties as factual accuracy need not concern us.

1 To begin with, I simply photographed a phone with the receiver off the hook. By placing it on its side, a small sense of chaos is already achieved. I chose a phone with the keypad in the receiver so that I'd have the base free on which to place the Energis logo afterwards.

4 The interiors of the base and the handset were drawn and filled with a flat color to fill the gaps where the tops had been broken off. This was simply a matter of inventing the new shapes using the Pen tool to draw the smoothly curved outlines.

7 The speaker is simply a loudspeaker from a stereo system, photographed and distorted to fit; the printed circuit board is actually a computer logic board cut to fit the interior of the phone.

8 Opposite is the finished illustration, with background and shading added. The Energis logo was taken from their website and redrawn, then distorted using the Shear tool; the shading was added using the Emboss feature in Layer Effects.

2 The first step was to separate the two halves of both the receiver and the handset, exactly as shown in the television example on the previous spread. While it would also have been possible to break the handset into shattered fragments, it adds to the sense of realism if the constituent parts remain intact. If you (or your children) have ever tried to break a telephone handset, you'll know how resilient they can be.

3 Each button was isolated using QuickMask, and then cut to a new layer using Shift ⌘ J Shift ctrl J. The button background was recreated, and then the buttons rearranged individually.

Outlining the buttons was the trickiest part of this illustration. It would have taken too long using the Pen tool: instead, I entered QuickMask mode and used a hard-edged brush of the same diameter as the end of a button. Clicking at one end, then holding *Shift* and clicking at the other end, drew a smooth lozenge that exactly fitted the shape of each button. If you're using a graphics tablet, this method will only work if you have pressure sensitivity turned off.

5 To make the interiors look more realistic, shading was added using the Burn tool to give a sense of depth and roundness. The horizontal ridges inside the back of the handset were added because the flat interior looked too dull without them.

6 The disk covering the mouthpiece was cut to a new layer, and both the disk and the hole given depth using the techniques described in Chapter 9.

Chaos and complexity

1 The student was clearly going to be the key figure in this image, so it was important to find the right one. Many royalty-free photographs of people are shot from up a ladder; this one had enough action to make him appear to be struggling with his task.

WHEN AN IMAGE IS TO BE PRINTED right across a spread, it can help to pack a lot of detail into it. This illustration for the student magazine Juice showed a student struggling to write his curriculum vitae (résumé) amid the chaos of his untidy living quarters.

I decided on the top-down view of this illustration simply to add dynamism to it: plus, I knew I had a picture of a desk and chair viewed from above. All the other props were either photographed or distorted to fit.

4 The next major props were the computer, the trash basket and the guitar. The guitar was given depth, and the desk drawer opened, using the techniques described in the first two sections of Chapter 9. With the big stuff in position, I could place the smaller items.

IMAGES: STOCKBYTE, HEMERA, PHOTODISC

2 The desk and chair were the next major props. Originally the chair was facing the desk, but it didn't take much to move it; the only constraint was positioning it so that its perspective matched that of the rest of the scene. The props on the desk were too business-oriented, but they'd all be covered up later.

3 The carpet was simply a scan of a piece of wallpaper cut to an irregular shape. The image needed a solid base, but I didn't want to square it to maintain the visual interest of the scene. I also changed the student's expression using the Goo filter (see Chapter 11), and recolored his T shirt.

Creating an irregular outline for an illustration is an easy way to add life to the image when it's printed: this is far more appealing on the page than a squared-up picture would have been. The key is knowing which elements need to be included, such as the carpet, and which can be missed out: I originally put a wall behind the desk, but removed it when it became clear it wasn't needed.

5 All the other props were added and positioned where they fitted best. You need a fairly comprehensive library of images in order to find all these elements; most of them came from the Hemera Photo-Objects 50,000 collection.

6 The final stage, as ever, was to add the shadows. These were created on several layers – one above the carpet, one grouped with the top of the desk, and so on. There's no point adding shadows until the composition is more or less complete, since they can be awkward to edit afterwards.

The fall of the house of cards

1 The Dimensions model showed the formation of a completed house of cards. While this wouldn't be used in the finished illustration, it made a useful template to show where to place the cards themselves.

MAKING THIS HOUSE OF CARDS appear to be in the process of collapse – while still looking like a house of cards – meant that each card had to be carefully placed to show it in the act of falling.

The illustration was for The Guardian, relating to an article about the demise of energy company Enron. Their distinctive logo, placed on the back of each card, tied the illustration to the story.

In this instance I made the original card house model in Dimensions (see Chapter 9), a simple task which took just a few minutes to put together. This formed the template around which the cards were built.

4 A few cards were added that break out of the line of the template. At the bottom of the pile, the cards were only slightly disarrayed: any misalignment here would cause more chaos higher up the stack. Each card was simply distorted to look as if it was falling.

2 The Enron logo was placed on a card-shaped background, drawn with the Shapes tool. The patterned area outside the logo was filled with a cross-hatch pattern that I created for drawing fences, and colored.

3 The first few cards were put in place, following the template. Each card was distorted using Free Transform to fit the template and placed behind the card in front of it: it was easier to work from the front backwards.

5 With all the cards in place, the template could be hidden so that we can see the full effect. No shading has been added yet, although the cards were given some thickness by selecting each one and holding ⌥ *alt* as it was nudged up and right a couple of pixels.

6 Each card was shaded using the Burn tool to add realism to the scene. In addition, the falling cards were duplicated and rotated, and their opacity reduced: those at the top were set to 30% opacity, reducing to just 10% at the bottom of the stack.

HOT TIP

Using a simple modeling program such as Dimensions can greatly help in the placement of objects in a 3D environment, even when the template is discarded at the end. Matching this sort of perspective viewpoint would have been a much trickier task if the cards had all simply been placed by eye: I know this to be true, since this was the way I originally attempted to do the illustration.

SHORTCUTS
MAC WIN BOTH

223

The cover of this book . . .

EACH CHAPTER IN THIS book has dealt with a separate technique. In the real world, however, a single montage may easily combine many different skills to make the image work.

By way of conclusion, we'll look at how the cover of this book was put together over the next six pages. All of the techniques used here have been described earlier in the book.

The aim of the cover was twofold: firstly, it had to be an appealing advertisement for the book. This is the prime difference between illustration and pure art; illustration serves a commercial purpose – in this case, to sell the book – whereas art can stand on its own to be appreciated or reviled, as the case may be.

Secondly, the cover was intended to look at first glance like a photograph but, on closer inspection, it should have been clear to the reader that it could not be a single photographic image. The figure's head, created in Poser, was chosen to accentuate that sense of unreality.

1 The original photograph for the body was taken in my studio. Because I was lit by tungsten lamps, the daylight from the window formed a bluish tint on my shirt.

2 Cut out from the background, I flipped the figure and cut off the near hand. It would have been impossible to get it in focus; some things are better done by montage.

6 The desk was darkened using Curves so that the reflections added later would stand out. Layer masks on the body and hand were used to make them fit together better.

7 Not my Apple Cinema Display, sadly, but a test computer at the offices of MacUser. Remember to carry your digital camera with you whenever you go out!

11 Poser hair is never particularly convincing; this hair was taken from another photograph, and distorted to fit the Poser head (whose eyebrows were recolored to match).

12 The glass was modeled in Dimensions in two halves by rotating its profile around 180°. Here's the back half put into place on the desktop.

3 I photographed my hand lit from below, so that the shadows would appear on the back of it. When placed in the montage, it would look as if the tools were emanating light.

4 When the first two elements were montaged together it was clear that the hand didn't fit the body. It doesn't matter: the glass of tools would cover up any ugly joins.

5 The desk was drawn with the Pen tool, and filled with my standard wooden texture. I positioned it behind the body so that the far hand, also behind the body, would overlap it.

8 The monitor and keyboard fit neatly into the montage. I'd already cut the far hand and arm to a new layer, moving it behind the body so I could position it independently.

9 The head was created in Poser (see Chapter 9), using the Michael 2 model from Daz3d. Released just days before the artwork was completed, this model has great realism.

10 A layer mask was applied to the head to blend it smoothly into the body, and a little shading was added to the neck of the original body to make the head sit more comfortably.

HOT TIP

Splitting an object such as this glass into two halves is an easy way to turn it into a container. It's a technique that can be applied to many different kinds of objects, and is particularly suited to those created in a 3D application.

13 The front half of the glass. By splitting it into two, I would be able to place all the tools inside the glass by positioning them between the two glass layers.

14 The Plastic Wrap filter turned the dull surface of the glass into something far more shiny. A bluish tint was added, and the contrast increased overall.

15 The opacity of the glass was reduced to 70% so that we could see both the background through it and the tools inside it. We can also see the inside of the base.

...the cover of this book...

16 The objects – all 'real' versions of Photoshop tools – were added one by one between the two glass layers. Because the front glass was set to a 70% opacity, we can see the tools through it.

17 The Eyedropper tool was also modeled in Dimensions, and split into two pieces: the bulb was used at 100% opacity, whereas the tube's opacity was lowered slightly to make it transparent.

18 The airbrush and magnifying glass were added next. The lens from the magnifying glass was cut out and made into a separate layer – it's not shown in this step.

  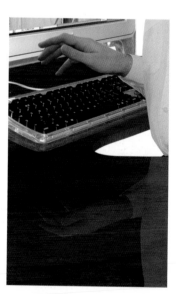

22 The desk was given some thickness by duplicating the shape of the edge and filling the new shape with the same wood texture, this time rotated so that the grain runs vertically.

23 To make the reflection of the keyboard, I simply duplicated it, sent it behind the original keyboard and lowered its opacity. It wasn't necessary to flip it vertically to achieve the effect.

24 The body and hand were both duplicated and flipped, and their opacity reduced. The hand needed to be moved to a new position relative to the body to make the reflected perspective work.

19 The lens was added back at a low opacity, so that it shaded the view through it. Much later, we'd make the glass magnify, but that needed to wait until the montage had acquired a background.

20 The pencil was simply added into the mix; the lasso was drawn using the Nowhouse Propeller filter (see Chapter 11) and a mask added so it could be hidden where it wrapped around the pencil.

21 The bandage, representing the Healing tool in Photoshop 7, was drawn by filling a round-ended rectangle with an array of dots; it was curved using the Shear tool, and shaded using Dodge and Burn.

HOT TIP

Reflections in shiny surfaces go a long way towards making montages look more realistic. But when combining the reflections of multiple objects, as in this case, wait until all the objects are in their final position before adding their reflections to avoid a lot of fiddling about later.

25 The monitor was also duplicated and flipped. When simply overlaid on top of the other elements, it can be seen through them: but it needed to be hidden where it intersects the hand and keyboard.

26 I added a layer mask to the keyboard reflection, and loaded the reflected keyboard and hand opacity by holding ⌘ *ctrl* and clicking on their layer names. These regions were then masked out.

27 I'd already added the new screen to the monitor by taking a screen capture of an earlier stage of the artwork; this was then added to the reflected monitor in the standard manner.

SHORTCUTS
MAC | WIN | BOTH

...the cover of this book

28 Here's the full montage so far. While it's a crisp image when viewed on a plain white background, it loses all sense of realism; what's needed is a background that will add a sense of place to the montage without detracting from the main focal point.

29 The shadows of all the elements in the montage were made by making a new shadow layer, then holding ⌘ *Shift* *ctrl* *Shift* and clicking on each layer's name in turn to add their outline to the selection. This was then filled with black, blurred and reduced in opacity.

32 With the background in place, I could now finish the interior of the magnifying glass. First, I hid all the layers in front of the rim, and hid the lens itself; I selected the lens area, and made a merged copy of the background using ⌘ *Shift* *C* *ctrl* *Shift* *C*. I wasn't worried about losing that fiddly bulb of the airbrush.

33 With the lens area still selected, I pasted the merged copy into it by selecting Paste Into (⌘ *Shift* *V* *ctrl* *Shift* *V*). This placed the copied area onto a new layer with an unlinked layer mask; I could now enlarge the copied region independently of the mask, so its visibility was constrained to that area.

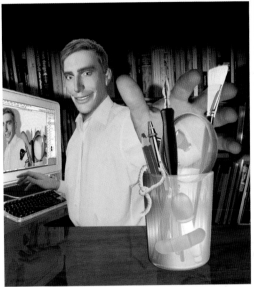

30 After toying with several different backgrounds, I ended up with this head-on view of a bookcase. This provided the visual interest I wanted without conflicting with the main image.

31 The shading at the top was added by making a new layer, and using the Gradient tool set to Foreground to Transparent to make a simple fade from black at the top to nothing. Holding the **Shift** key while using the tool constrained the movement to vertical.

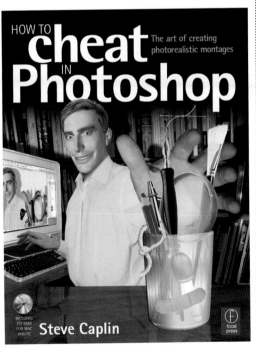

34 Next, I placed the original lens back in position at a reduced opacity so that it added a gloss to the pasted copy. This may all seem like rather a long-winded way of achieving a minor task, but the montage would have looked less convincing without it. The devil, as they say, is in the detail.

35 Finally, I added a layer mask to the word 'Photoshop' so that the hair stood in front of it.

HOT TIP

It may seem strange to create a montage from the front backwards, rather than beginning with a scene and then populating it. This, after all, is how a photographer would proceed. But in Photoshop we have the luxury of being able to work in our own way; and the best results usually come from making the focus of the image work first, and adding a background at the end.

SHORTCUTS
MAC WIN BOTH

229

Photomontage ethics

A COUPLE OF YEARS AGO the issue of photomontage was brought into question when a photograph of prominent left-wing politician, on a night out with his wife, appeared in a London newspaper. In front of him on the table were a couple of bottles of beer, the kind that has a foil-wrapped cap. Someone at the newspaper had enlarged one of the beer bottles so that it looked like a bottle of champagne – a deception magnified by the headline 'Champagne Socialist' that proclaimed his decadence.

As distortion of the truth goes, it seemed like a minor infraction. But the issue made national news. I was interviewed about it on radio, and asked whether I condoned this sort of underhand trickery. I pointed out that, had the photographer merely rearranged the scene, moving one of the bottles to the foreground so that it obscured less of the politician in question, there would have been no debate; yet the results would have been identical. It's only because the change was made in the cold light of the newspaper offices that it caused an outrage. That's all very well, opined the interviewer, but how would I feel if he took the interview he'd just done with me and rearranged it back at the studio to suit his own purposes? But that, I pointed out, was exactly his intention: he was going to boil down 40 minutes of interview into a five minute segment, choosing the parts that told the story he wanted to tell. My comment never made it into the final broadcast.

There's a lot of confusion about photomontage, much of it stemming from the misconception that photographs somehow tell the truth, as if there's an absolute truth out there that can be captured in one-sixtieth of a second; any tinkering with that truth must be a lie.

But photographs don't tell the truth any more than words. The photographer may take several rolls of film, each frame capturing a slice of time; the photo editor will then choose the picture that tells the story his newspaper wants told. The sub-editor may then crop the picture to fit the space available, and in doing so will again retell the story.

The photograph above left shows an idyllic view of a small cottage, set amid verdant foliage. But it's a lie: the picture has been cropped from the original image, above right, which tells a very different story. Anyone who had rented this as a holiday home after seeing it on a website would have every right to feel cheated by the reality: and yet there's been no Photoshop trickery involved, simply a selective decision about how much of the 'truth' to tell.

We may take a roll of film on holiday, from which we choose half a dozen to go in the album. The rest are discarded – one person has their eyes closed, the expression isn't so appealing, a tourist got into shot in the background. Yet we are just as guilty of editing the truth as if we'd montaged the elements together in Photoshop: we're telling the story we want told.

I once argued this point with a photographer who had just produced an image of newly released hostage John McCarthy outside his home, with a rainbow glistening in the sky behind him. He'd had to wait all day for the right image, he told me, and just caught the rainbow in time. But, I said somewhat facetiously, I could have put the rainbow there for you and saved you the trouble. He was horrified: his picture was the 'real thing'. And yet John McCarthy doesn't run outdoors every time a rainbow appears: this image was as contrived as if I'd montaged it myself.

I'm not saying there aren't limits to what should be done with photomontage. But if obvious montages make more people realize that the camera nearly always lies, then the world will be a better place.

EyeCandy 4000

Andromeda 3D

Nowhouse
Propeller

Flaming Pear

Kai's Power Tools

11 Carry on spending

Powerful though Photoshop is, there are some effects you simply can't achieve with the built-in tools and filters. Over the years a number of third party developers have brought out plug-in filters that enhance the potential of Photoshop in some way: some are useful, everyday tools, others are weird and amusing but have little practical application.

Because this book deals with reproducing reality, I'm only going to look at the filters which offer specifically real-world effects. Included in this section are my personal favorites; some are from major graphics corporations such as Corel, others are shareware offerings made by one person and sold through a website. Very often, it's the one-off filters that provide the most useful functionality, and some of the filters that few people have heard of are the most useful enabling tools there are.

EyeCandy 4000

EYECANDY 4000 is the successor to EyeCandy 3, and is a suite of plug-in tools that offers a wide range of real-world effects. Where many plug-in developers concentrate on the weird and the wacky, EyeCandy specializes in tools that simulate reality.

The most immediately impressive filter in the set is Chrome, which can turn any object into gleaming metal that can be fully customized to resemble a variety of surfaces. Custom bevels can be drawn to suit any purpose, as well as chosen from the wide range of presets that come with the product.

But EyeCandy can also create such difficult effects as fire, smoke and water drops with surprisingly good results; it also has the ability to make selections drip and melt in a convincing and appealing way.

The interface is simple but comprehensive, with separate panes for controlling every aspect of each filter. Previews are as large as you want them to be, since you can enlarge the window to fill your monitor – although the larger the window, the longer complex effects will take to preview. Most useful of all is the Random Seed button, which changes the way the effect is applied while retaining all the parameters you've set: it's easy to keep clicking the button, changing the effect slightly each time, until you get precisely the effect you want.

Manufacturer: Alien Skin Software

URL: www.alienskin.com

HOW TO USE IT

1 Begin by setting up your type, and rendering it as a layer (EyeCandy can't work with type layers). Here, we've applied the Drip filter to make the type look as if it's melting.

2 A second application of the Drip filter makes the distortion look more random. By changing the parameters, I've made larger drips that are more widely spaced. The ability to build up multiple effects by varying a filter makes EyeCandy far more flexible.

3 Now, that dripping metal is taken into the Chrome filter. This allows us to set any bevel size and type we want, as well as specifying both the type of metal (determined by the image reflected in it) and the surface properties. By adding a 'flaw' to the surface, we make it ripple.

Adds random curling to the individual flames   100%

4 Next up comes the Fire filter. There are several ways of applying this, and it's possible to generate convincing flames by choosing the right method. Here, I've set flames to start at the far edge of the selected object, rising almost vertically.

5 The Smoke filter works in much the same way as the Fire, but creates wispy streams that really do look like smoke. Of course, it's possible to change the color and type of the smoke to represent just about any flowing material you want to reproduce.

6 Here's the finished image, with all the filters applied cumulatively. It's the kind of illustration that would have taken hours to produce by conventional means, and still wouldn't have looked half as good. Buy EyeCandy for the Chrome filter alone, then find out what else it will do.

Andromeda 3D

ANDROMEDA make a range of filters, including a specialized filter that creates engraving-style line artwork from grayscale photographs. For the graphic artist, though, the plug-in of choice is their 3D filter.

Andromeda 3D has the ability to wrap a Photoshop layer around a sphere, cube or cylinder, or to place it on an infinite plane. The image can be tiled, so that it repeats endlessly: this is useful both for making planes from regular artwork, and for wrapping images around other surfaces.

The filter is reasonably fast in operation, and is capable of excellent results – crisp, clear images that have the additional options of lighting and shading, as well as the ability to denote a dropout color that will render transparently.

Andromeda 3D does have a couple of drawbacks, though. Firstly, the interface is so mathematical that it seems almost impenetrable for the novice user: there's a lot to get used to before you start to feel confident with all its functions.

The other problem is that images are rendered in the same space that holds the base artwork. This means if you want to end up with a square image, you need to distort your artwork to square to make it work. It's an irritating constraint to an otherwise useful plug-in.

Manufacturer: Andromeda Software, Inc

URL: www.andromeda.com

HOW TO USE IT

1 Any single layer can be used as the base artwork for wrapping using the Andromeda 3D filter. The problem is that the artwork has to be precisely the same size as the space the image is rendered into, which can be a limiting factor.

2 The artwork appears in the filter wrapped around the surface of your choice – but you need to hit the Preview button to see it rendered in the small preview window.

3 By scaling the photograph, you can make it fit the size of the surface you're mapping it onto. You can also choose to tile it, so that it wraps all the way around.

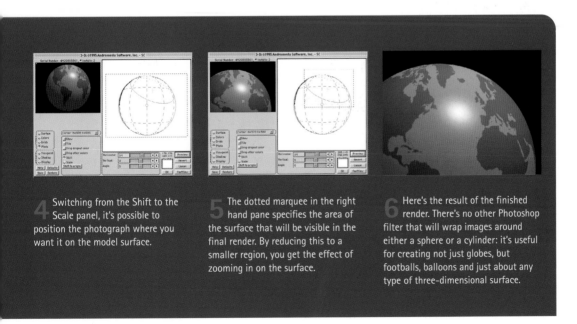

4 Switching from the Shift to the Scale panel, it's possible to position the photograph where you want it on the model surface.

5 The dotted marquee in the right hand pane specifies the area of the surface that will be visible in the final render. By reducing this to a smaller region, you get the effect of zooming in on the surface.

6 Here's the result of the finished render. There's no other Photoshop filter that will wrap images around either a sphere or a cylinder: it's useful for creating not just globes, but footballs, balloons and just about any type of three-dimensional surface.

Nowhouse Propeller

NOWHOUSE PROPELLER is a unique plug-in that allows Photoshop users to turn any object into a brush. This makes it easy to add ropes, chains, and phone cables to fit any curve or shape you want: simply paint them into the artwork.

Even though it's still at version 1.0, Propeller offers a huge degree of sophistication and user control. As well as being able to determine the size of each brush as you use it, the Dynamics tab allows you to specify a range of variations. You can make it simply follow the direction in which you paint, as seen in the rope example in the main screen shot; you can also set it to operate with a uniform angle, a technique used for the film strip. It's also possible to make the thickness and color of the brushstroke vary with the pressure or tilt if you have a graphics tablet, or with the speed of brushing if you don't; you can even set the brush to twirl as you paint.

Propeller comes with a wide range of brushes, including organic forms that allow you to paint plants and trees, as well as real objects such as cord, chains and beads.

Perhaps the most exciting aspect of Propeller is its ability to enable the user to define custom brushes, and it's this aspect that I've outlined in the workthrough below.

It's not a well-known tool, but Propeller ranks high on my list of essential add-ons.

Manufacturer: Nowhouse

URL: www.nowhouse.com

HOW TO USE IT

1 Begin by choosing the object you want to turn into a brush. Here, I've photographed a piece of rope, and cut a section that will join at either end. The next step is to make the join work seamlessly.

2 Make a copy of the rope layer, and offset both in opposite directions so that the two ends now meet in the middle. As you can see, there's a discrepancy between the two that we need to sort out.

3 Using the Clone tool, fix the join so that the two ends of the rope match together perfectly. You don't need to worry about the left and right ends – they're sure to fit, because of the way they were duplicated.

4 The next step is to make an Alpha channel that defines the visible area of the rope. It's this channel that Propeller will use to generate the transparency around the brush. Save the finished image as a TIFF file, and place it in the Patterns folder within the Propeller folder.

5 You can now define a new brush in the Propeller dialog, and begin painting with it straight away. The rope will follow the curves you draw with the brush, bending smoothly along them as you paint.

6 If you wish, you can change all the parameters of your object: you can vary the size, change the color, and even make the width of the painted stroke vary with the speed or pressure with which you draw.

Flaming Pear

DESPITE BEING ESSENTIALLY a one-man outfit, Flaming Pear have generated many useful filters over the years. These shareware plug-ins each perform a single task, and usually do so to perfection.

Flood, shown in the screenshot (right), has the ability to submerge any scene: in the preview seen here, the water is entirely artificial. Flood offers a high degree of user control, including the facility to set such parameters as the perspective, altitude, waviness, complexity and brilliance of the water.

A useful extra touch is the ability to be able to set a pond ripple on the water's surface. Simply click the preview at the point you want the ripple – it may be where you plan to place a boat, for example – and the ripple will appear. You can also set the size, height and undulation of the ripple.

Flood works best with images shot head-on, since the horizon line is always horizontal. This makes it difficult to work with scenes photographed at an angle, although it is possible to build up multiple reflective effects from each object in a montage and then blend them together.

Some of Flaming Pear's other filters, described below, continue the natural elements theme, allowing the creation of stars, planets and suns; others offer interesting bevel effects.

Manufacturer: Flaming Pear Software

URL: www.flamingpear.com

OTHER FLAMING PEAR FILTERS

1 Solar Cell generates vivid suns, with definable flares, spikes, haloes and bows. But reduce the radius of the sun to zero, and it makes great explosions.

2 Lunar Cell creates fantasy moons and planets of every imaginable kind. With an internet connection, it can even display current cloud data!

3 SuperBladePro offers the best beveling tools around. Turn any selection into glittering jewelry, customized with a huge range of parameters.

4 Glitterato is the solution for making star fields, complete with two nebula generators if you want them. A perfect companion to Lunar Cell.

Kai's Power Tools

KAI'S POWER TOOLS are not so much the granddaddy of all filters as the slightly peculiar uncle from the tropics who you wouldn't leave alone with the children. The inventor of the wacky interface, Kai Krause has created several sets of filters that range from the incredibly useful to the downright absurd.

The main screen shot here shows KPT Goo, a component of the KPT6 filter set – and four other filters from this set are shown below.

Previously a standalone application, Goo offers distortion techniques similar to those now built into Photoshop's Liquify filter, but simpler to use and generating much smoother results. In Goo, you simply brush pixels around where you want them to go: it's like using a far more powerful Smudge tool, but one that allows more controllable strokes along with more powerful features.

Goo also has the ability to create movies from the distortions you create: you simply drop a frame you like into the Animation strip, and Goo will generate smooth, flowing movies that blend between each step.

KPT Goo is the best tool for creating caricatures, but is also capable of making fine adjustments to allow your photographs to display a wide emotional range simply by tweaking the position of the mouth and eyebrows.

Manufacturer: Corel

URL: www.corel.com

OTHER KPT FILTERS

1 KPT Gel is a tool for painting with treacle or liquid metal. Its variety of tools allow a range of special effects to be applied, to create dynamic three-dimensional artwork.

2 LensFlare takes Photoshop's built-in filter and adds a huge range of lens types, refraction techniques and special effects. It's also fun to use.

3 Projector allows any Photoshop layer to be tiled and viewed as if it were laid on a three-dimensional plane. Unlike Andromeda 3D, it won't wrap around curved surfaces.

4 Sky Effects generates skies, complete with sun and moon if you want them. The effects are only semi-realistic, but it's a good way of getting the sky you want.

Where page references in multiple-number entries are shown in **bold type**, this indicates a page or section in which particular attention is paid to this subject.

What's on the CD

 This symbol, which appears throughout the book, indicates that you'll find a Photoshop file on the CD to accompany the workthrough detailed in that section. The files are in a folder called Chapter Files, and each one includes all the elements of the starting point for each workthrough so that you can try the techniques out for yourself. Each Photoshop file on the CD contains a note outlining the task you're supposed to complete.

 This symbol indicates that, in addition to the Photoshop file, there's also a QuickTime movie on the CD that shows the workthrough played out in real time. I've included movies where there's some benefit to being able to see the artwork being created 'live'; sometimes it's easier to understand a concept when it's played out for you rather than just by reading about it. The movies are located in the folder called Quicktime Movies.

The folder named Demo Software includes demonstration versions of several of the third party plug-ins that I've discussed in Chapter 11 (in both Mac and Windows formats), as well as demo versions of Poser and Adobe Dimensions (both discussed in Chapter 9). The demo versions are all designed to show you the full capabilities of the filters, and most are save-disabled to prevent you from applying the effects to real artwork. The demos are saved in .sit or .zip format; you'll need a third party utility such as Stuffit or WinZip to decompress them so you can install them onto your hard disk. To try out the plug-in filters, you'll need to install them into the Plug-ins folder inside the Photoshop folder on your hard disk.

The CD also includes a selection of royalty-free images from StockByte, which you're free to use in your artwork. And there's also a demonstration version of Hemera Photo-Objects which includes 500 images from their collection.

Also available from Focal Press ...

Adobe Photoshop 7.0 for Photographers
Martin Evening

A professional image editor's guide to the creative use of Photoshop for the Macintosh and PC.

Martin Evening's award-winning Adobe Photoshop for Photographers titles have become must-have reference sources - the only Photoshop books written to deal directly with the needs of photographers. Whether you are an accomplished user or are just starting out, this book contains a wealth of practical advice, hints and tips to help you achieve professional-looking results.

Adobe Photoshop 7.0 for Photographers begins with an introduction to working with digital images, providing essential, up-to-date information on everything from scanning devices to color management and output issues.

- Benefit from Martin Evening's experience as an Alpha tester and official Adobe roadshow speaker for Photoshop 7.0

- Includes free CD-ROM containing invaluable movie tutorials and a selection of images to experiment with

Reviews of *Adobe Photoshop 6.0 for Photographers*

'Someone has just re-written the bible, the Photoshop bible...Whether you are an expert or a beginner, this is a book that talks your language.'
Digital PhotoFX

'A mine of useful information, aimed at not only helping photographers to produce the very best quality images, but also gives techniques for image manipulation. For anyone involved with image processing this is a must have book!'
Photo Technique

'This publication is a must for all photographers, independent of your level of experience with the package, as it's written by a practising professional photographer with you, the photographer, in mind.'
The Association of Photographers

ISBN 0240516907 • July 2002 • £29.99

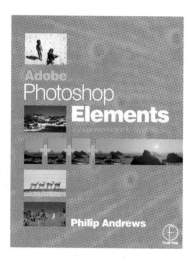

Also available from Focal Press ...

Photoshop 6.0 A-Z
Peter Bargh

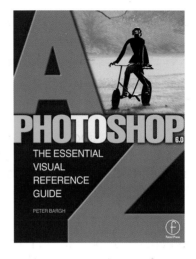

This quick, easy reference text is a must-have purchase for every Photoshop user. It is one of a kind – giving an easily accessible visual guide to all those vital Photoshop terms. Keep it next to your computer screen. It is a constant reference that will save you hours of frustration when the meaning of that term is on the tip of your tongue.

- Save valuable time with this clear and easy to use A to Z guide to Photoshop
- Covers all versions from 3.0 to 6.0
- Full colour images for easy guidance are used throughout
- Relevant for you whether you are a MAC or PC user

Peter Bargh was technical writer for *Practical Photography* magazine and Editor of *Buying Cameras*. He launched *Digital PhotoFX* magazine in 1997 and edited it until recently, when he left to set up his own company, Magezine Publishing Ltd. Peter is now publishing *ePHOTOzine*, a web based magazine, that will increase Internet presence for photography.

Reviews of *Photoshop 5.5 A-Z*

'...this handy and simple-to-use paperback...is a perfect adjunct to...any other technique book dealing with Photoshop.'
Professional Photographer

'There are stacks of guide books on Photoshop and I'd feared this would be another that is useful but impossible to navigate. The reality was a pleasant surprise, with the author honestly appraising some of the more esoteric features... of all the Photoshop self-help guides I've come across, Peter Bargh's book is the easiest to use.'
Amateur Photographer

ISBN 0240516559 • April 2001 • £15.99

Also available from Focal Press ...

Max Ferguson's Digital Darkroom Masterclass

Max Ferguson

- Learn from a professional how to get your creative photofinishing techniques up to scratch!

These unique masterclasses, in the modern technique-led approach to photographic post-production, show how darkroom and digital techniques go hand in hand in finishing off an image. Max provides, among many others, a thorough explanation of: split grade printing, printing through stockings, monochrome toning emulation. So you too can achieve professional-looking results, a number of images are shown with a breakdown of the methods used in their production.

The accompanying CD-ROM contains: a series of tutorials for monitor viewing; some of the author's images in layered form for readers to edit and manipulate; extra information on colour management as PDFs; and relevant downloads from Adobe.

'I will buy anything by Max Ferguson... This is a book I want to read and I would imagine that the majority of those involved in darkroom or digital printing would too.'
Adam Woolfitt – professional digital imaging photographer; founding member of the Digital Imaging Group, London

ISBN 0240515692 • Sept 2000 • £29.99

To order your copy call +44 (0)1865 888180 (UK) or +1 800 366 2665 (USA) or visit the Focal Press website: www.focalpress.com

Also available from Focal Press ...

Creative After Effects 5.0
Angie Taylor

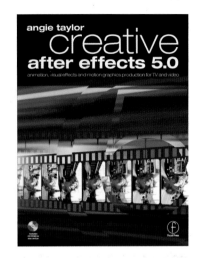

- Unique book and CD package shows you how to get the best out of After Effects 5.0

- Project based tutorials help you develop and apply your skills

In this dynamic new text Angie Taylor provides a comprehensive guide to the fundamental workings of After Effects, explaining how to think creatively with the software, so that you can achieve the most unique and professional-looking results. Also included are lots of invaluable tips, tricks, ideas, animation rules, design and typography rules and details of other resources you will find useful.

The free CD-ROM provides the necessary files to complete each tutorial in the book, as well as a plethora of free fonts, footage, plugins and demo software.

If you are a designer already using After Effects and want to improve and reconfirm your working methods, brush up on your creative skills, and improve your graphic and animation techniques, or if you simply need to learn After Effects from scratch, then this is the book for you.

'Angie Taylor is the best After Effects teacher I know. She goes beyond technical descriptions of features, and shows you how best to use them in real-world projects.'
Bruce Bullis, Senior API Engineer, Adobe Dynamic Media, Adobe Systems Inc.

'Angie Taylor's work is inspired. She is a highly creative animator – inventive, witty and naturally sympathetic to individual programme's styles.'
Carys Edwards, Director, Children's BBC

ISBN 0240516222 • August 2001 • £27.50

To order your copy call +44 (0)1865 888180 (UK) or +1 800 366 2665 (USA) or visit the Focal Press website: www.focalpress.com

Focal Press

www.focalpress.com

Join Focal Press on-line
As a member you will enjoy the following benefits:

- an email bulletin with **information on new books**
- a regular **Focal Press Newsletter**:
    - o   featuring a selection of new titles
    - o   keeps you informed of **special offers, discounts and freebies**
    - o   alerts you to **Focal Press news and events** such as author signings and seminars
- complete access to **free content** and reference material on the focalpress site, such as the focalXtra articles and commentary from our authors
- a **Sneak Preview** of selected titles (sample chapters) *before* they publish
- a chance to have your say on our **discussion boards** and **review books** for other Focal readers

Focal Club Members are invited to give us feedback on our products and services.
Email: worldmarketing@focalpress.com – we want to hear your views!

Membership is **FREE**. To join, visit our website and register. If you require any further information regarding the on-line club please contact:

Lucy Lomas-Walker
Email: lucy.lomas-walker@repp.co.uk
Tel: +44 (0) 1865 314438
Fax: +44 (0)1865 314572
Address: Focal Press, Linacre House,
Jordan Hill, Oxford, UK, OX2 8DP

Catalogue

For information on all Focal Press titles, our full catalogue is available online at www.focalpress.com and all titles can be purchased here via secure online ordering, or contact us for a free printed version:

USA
Email: christine.degon@bhusa.com
Tel: +1 781 904 2607

Europe and rest of world
Email: jo.coleman@repp.co.uk
Tel: +44 (0)1865 314220

Potential authors

If you have an idea for a book, please get in touch:

USA
editors@focalpress.com

Europe and rest of world
focal.press@repp.co.uk